Glass
and Glassware

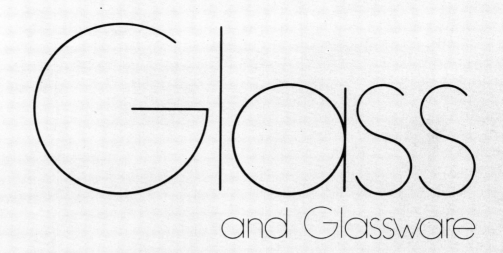

George Savage

Glass
and Glassware

Cathay Books

This edition published 1978 by
Cathay Books
59 Grosvenor Street
London W1

© 1973 Hennerwood Publications Limited

ISBN 0 904644 62 6

Produced by Mandarin Publishers Limited
22a Westlands Road
Quarry Bay, Hong Kong

Printed in Hong Kong

Contents

The Techniques of Glassmaking

Glass is an unusual substance. It belongs to a small group termed supercooled liquids, which means that it passes from the molten to the rigid state without a change of structure. It is also termed amorphous, because it is not crystalline in its structure, unlike the natural hardstone, rock crystal, which it otherwise resembles. Chemically, it can be regarded as a complex silicate of the metallic elements present. Glass is made from silica in one form or another, usually sand, with the addition of a variety of alkaline fluxes such as soda, potash, and lime, and sometimes of lead oxide. These promote the fusion of the silica, and confer on the glass properties which are more or less peculiar to the type of flux employed.

Soda glass is the product of sand and sodium carbonate; in former times this was obtained from the ash of plants growing around the shores of the Mediterranean, such as seaweeds, or the Spanish plant, barilla, which grows in the salt marshes near Alicante. Spanish barilla was employed in England to make soda glass in the fourteenth century. Soda glass is light in weight, and, when heated, remains plastic and workable over a wider temperature range than other varieties, lending itself to such manipulative techniques as those used by the Venetians.

Potash glass is sometimes called *fern glass*, or *forest glass*, because it was fluxed with the ashes of inland plants such as ferns, which yield potassium carbonate. It was especially employed in Bohemia (now Czechoslovakia). Somewhat heavier than soda glass, it passes from the molten to the rigid state more quickly, and is therefore more difficult to manipulate into elaborate forms. It is, however, harder and more brilliant, and lends itself to such decorative techniques as facet cutting and wheel engraving, which are later described.

Lead glass, also called *flint glass*, to which lead was added in relatively large quantities, was first known in Roman times, but for all practical purposes it was a late seventeenth-century English development by George Ravenscroft. In its brilliance and suitability for facet cutting it exceeds potash glass. It is the heaviest of all glasses, and in the eighteenth century it was employed by Frédéric Strass to imitate such precious stones as the diamond in the making of 'paste' jewellery. It was also the glass used for the manufacture of eighteenth-century English and Irish cut glass.

In the nineteenth century many advances were made in glass technology, leading to the employment of new fluxes and novel methods of formation and decoration, and these are discussed in Chapter X. A great deal of glass was made by traditional methods, however, and even today these are still in use for all but the commonest wares of domestic utility.

At a sufficiently high temperature glass is a molten, fiery substance, but as it cools it reaches a state between the molten and rigid states in which it has a treacly consistency. This is soon lost in cooling but can be restored by heating, enabling various manipulative processes to be carried out over a relatively long period of time, especially in the case of soda glass.

There are two principal ways of forming objects of glass – moulding and blowing. Moulded glass vessels are made by pouring molten glass into a mould which is in the form of the exterior of the desired object, the interior being formed by a core. If the glass is blown into the mould a core is unnecessary. Some of the earliest glass was made in moulds filled with powdered glass which was subsequently fused by heating, and this practice was revived in the nineteenth century in the manufacture of the glass sometimes termed *pâte de verre*. Moulds were usually made of a refractory fireclay able to withstand the temperatures involved, or of stone or metal. Moulding preceded blowing, and the earliest blown glass vessels were blown into a mould, free-blowing being a later development. In modern times machines have been devised for doing this kind of work automatically, especially in the manufacture of bottles.

Glass blowing is a technique that demands a high degree of skill. When glass is in the plastic stage it can be gathered on the end of a long hollow tube and blown into a spherical bubble. All objects of blown glass start in this way, and by judicious reheating and continued blowing a large bubble of this kind can be formed. By swinging it at the end of the blowpipe a cylinder is produced. This was the first part of the technique once employed to make sheet glass (known as the *broad-glass process*). Then the hemispherical ends of the cylinder were cut off,

it was slit vertically, and finally reheated, opened out, and flattened into an oblong sheet.

Before the development of plate glass, sheet glass was also made by what is termed the *crown-glass technique*. A bubble of glass was blown. Then a rod was attached to the opposite side, and the blowpipe withdrawn. The bubble was then rotated vigorously in conjunction with judicious reheating until it assumed the form of a large flattened disc, which would end up about 50 inches in diameter. Page 11 shows an eighteenth-century workman rotating a disc of this kind, his hand protected from the heat by a metal shield. This technique is also sometimes termed the *Normandy process*.

Both the broad-glass and crown-glass methods could only provide small sheets, and large sheets for mirrors and windows did not exist till the end of the seventeenth century, when Bernard Perrot devised a method of casting glass on a flat copper bed. His invention led to the establishment of the Manufacture Royale des Grandes Glaces at Saint-Gobain, in Picardy, in 1693, and this still survives as one of the principal French manufactories. For many years this factory had a monopoly of the large sheets of glass used in the manufacture of the best quality mirrors, and plate glass was not in fact manufactured in England until towards the end of the eighteenth century.

In its plastic state glass can be cut with shears, and for most manipulative processes it is transferred from the blowpipe to what is termed the *pontil rod* (or *punty*). Page 10 illustrates a typical team of men in the act of making a wineglass. The master glassmaker, known as the *gaffer*, is sitting on the 'chair', which has arms projecting forwards on which the pontil can be rested and rotated. The wineglass in process of manufacture has been transferred from the blowpipe to the pontil, and has partially assumed the form of the finished object. The footmaker has collected glass to form the foot, and is helping the gaffer to attach it to the stem. The bowl, nearest to the gaffer, remains to be sheared off. In the background a boy carries a glass to the annealing furnace (the *lehr*, or *leer*) where glasses were reheated to disperse stresses in the material which had arisen during formation. Although this reconstruction from Pilkington's Glass Museum, Lancashire, is of an eighteenth-century team, the same general techniques are employed today in the production of handmade glass.

Soda glass, because of its plasticity, lends itself to a variety of decorative techniques which are not often attempted in either potash glass or lead glass. Trailing is an example. This is the attachment of softened glass rod to a vessel as a kind of ornament. It was commonly indented, and often impressed with patterns with the aid of pincers. In England towards the end of the seventeenth century glass rod was trailed round the exterior of some lead glass vessels, and then nipped together at intervals with pincers,

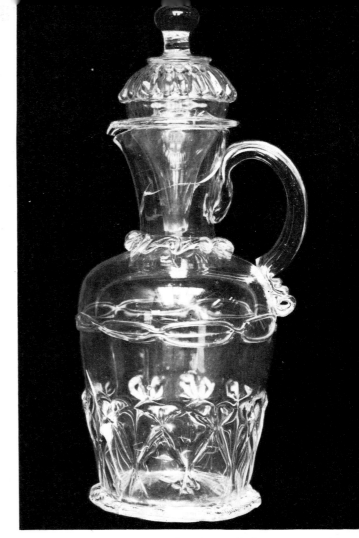

Opposite:
Pokal decorated with a hunting scene in matte and polished wheel engraving by Johann Christoph Kiessling, Dresden, *c.* 1730. Grinding and polishing mills driven by water power were set up in and around Dresden about 1700 for cutting both glass and semiprecious stones as part of the researches of Ehrenfried von Tschirnhausen into the making of porcelain and artificial semiprecious stones.

Right:
Decanter jug and stopper of lead glass 'nipt diamond waies' around the base, Ravenscroft period. In this example lead glass is still being employed in the manner of soda glass. Its particular properties of light refraction were not effectively used until facet cutting became widely adopted.

Below:
Bowl and cover decorated with cutting, late 18th century. This illustration shows very well the effect of light refraction which results from cutting lead glass into facets.

resulting in a series of diamond-shaped figures termed, at the time, 'nipt diamond waies' (nipped diamondwise). This was a revival of a Roman technique. At the beginning of the eighteenth century openwork baskets were first built up from glass rods by Venetian glass-workers. Much the same kind of work may have been done in Bristol about the same time. The Venetians, in the seventeenth century, employed glass rod, sometimes of more than one colour, to build up elaborate stems for goblets, which were pincered and manipulated into shape. These are often called 'winged' goblets. Glass rod in a variety of colours is also used in the manufacture of what is termed *millefiori* ('thousand flower') work, which is especially to be seen in the much sought after French paperweights. The technique was already ancient in Imperial Roman times, although the term itself dates only from the sixteenth century. At its simplest, the process involves fusing several differently coloured 'canes' or rods side by side so that, in section, they appear like a conventional flower. This rod is then treated like a stick of seaside rock and drawn out into a long, thin cane. A number of canes of different designs are then sliced transversely, and the sections are arranged side by side in the desired pattern and embedded in clear glass.

Particularly associated with Venice is a type of glass known as *latticinio*, which is decorated with threads of opaque white or coloured glass. Several techniques were employed, perhaps the simplest being the application of drawn-out threads to the surface of a vessel. White or coloured threads were sometimes picked up on a lump of molten glass (termed a *gather*) and then blown and manipulated into shape, which led to some distortion of the network. The more complex networks were made by first blowing a bubble, followed by collapsing one hemisphere into the other by sucking in a little air. This left a double walled vessel with threads crossing each other in a series of lozenges. The hemisphere could then be reheated and manipulated into the desired shape. By another method coloured glass rods were arranged round the interior of a cylindrical fireclay mould, which was filled with clear glass. The contents were then taken out, reheated, drawn out, and twisted. White and coloured twist stems for wineglasses were made in this way.

On Mohs' scale glass has a hardness of 5.5. This is slightly harder than ordinary steel, but much softer than sapphire, ruby, or emery (carborundum), and, of course, much softer than the diamond chips commonly employed to cut glass. The diamond is used to engrave ornament on glass of all kinds, and for this purpose it is mounted in a holder and employed either like a pencil (line engraving) or a chisel (stipple engraving). The technique of line engraving is very ancient, but stipple engraving first came into use in the Low Countries at the end of the seventeenth century (page 12).

In Roman times hardstones such as amethyst and agate were carved by abrading them with

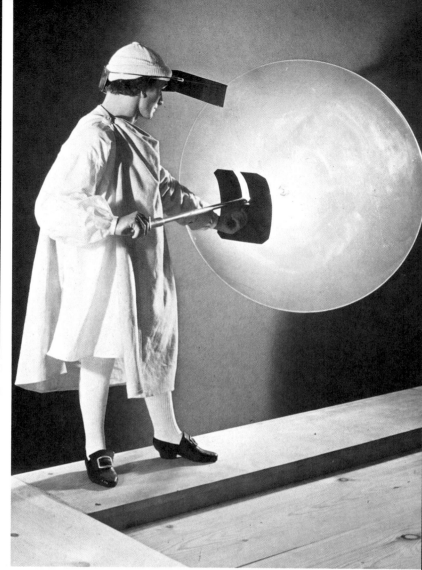

Opposite, above left :
Making a wineglass in the
18th century. The gaffer,
seated, trims the bowl with
shears. Behind him a com-
plete glass is taken to the
annealing chamber. The
stems of early glasses were
usually drawn out from the
base of the bowl, and the foot
added (drawn shank). Later,
the glass was made in three
parts—bowl, stem and foot—
welded together (stuck
shank).

Opposite, above right :
Spinning a disc of sheet glass
on the pontil in the 18th-
century manner. The spin-
ning would begin in the
mouth of the furnace with a
ring a few inches wide and
end as a disc as much as 50
inches across.

Opposite, bottom :
Glassworker's tools,
including tongs, shears and
callipers for measuring. The
basic equipment of the
vitrearius, along with the
blowpipe and the pontil, seen
in colour at right.

Above, left :
Glass blowing. The glass is
gathered on the end of a
hollow pipe and then blown
into a spherical bubble. This
is shaped by contact with
various tools, by rolling on a
table (the marver), or by
swinging it at the end of the
pipe to form a cylinder.

Above, right :
Wheel engraving. This
ancient technique depends on
the fact that a substance can
be cut by one that is harder.
Glass, with a hardness of 5·5
on Mohs' scale (where the
diamond is 10) can be en-
graved by abrading it with
sand carried on a rotating
wheel. Emery (carborun-
dum), with a hardness of 9, is
also used for this.

Below, right :
Working the glass while
plastic. With judicious
reheating soda glass especially
is extremely tolerant of
manipulation while soft.
Potash and lead glasses are
harder to work because of
their narrower temperature
range between ductility and
rigidity.

the aid of small rotating copper wheels charged with emery. The same technique was adapted to the decoration of Roman glass, of which some remarkable specimens have survived. The most widely known is the Portland Vase in the British Museum (page 24). This is a vase of dark-blue glass cased with opaque white glass. Cased glass (sometimes termed *overlay glass*) is glass of one colour which has been covered with a layer of another colour. The outer layer is then cut away in parts to reveal the colour beneath. In the case of the Portland Vase the white layer has been carved away to form an elaborate relief decoration of figures. Carving relief ornament of this kind is termed *cameo cutting*; patterns cut below the surface are termed *intaglio*, or, in German, *Hochschnitt* and *Tief-schnitt* respectively. The German terms are often employed because some exceptionally fine work of this kind was done in Bohemia in the seventeenth and eighteenth centuries.

Allied to cameo cutting is facet cutting, which is usually referred to as cut glass. Lead glass is normally employed for this purpose because of its high refractive index, that is to say, its power of higher refraction and reflection, in which it resembles to a lesser degree a cut diamond. The patterns into which this kind of glass is cut often resemble the faceting of a diamond, and each face collects light and reflects it at a different angle to that of its incidence. The brilliance of cut glass is partly due to the faceting, and partly to the qualities of the glass itself. Soda glass has rarely been cut in this way, except for a few untypical examples from eighteenth-century Venice; potash glass has more frequently been used for the purpose, especially in Bohemia. Lead glass has been employed for most work of this kind, particularly in England and Ireland.

Glass is coloured with a variety of metallic

Left, above:
Wineglass stipple engraved with a design of children playing by David Wolff, Holland, *c.* 1790. Stippling was a time-consuming technique which could hardly have been undertaken commercially; most of the stipple engravers, like the calligraphic engravers, were amateurs.

Left, below:
Goblet engraved by Elias Rosbach, Zechlin, *c.* 1740. Rosbach's working life continued until about 1765 and he moved from Zechlin to Berlin about 1742. A signed glass bears the inscription *Rosbach fecit Berlin*.

Below:
Plate with folded rim, decorated with white opposing spiral threads *(a reticelli)*, Venetian, 16th century. This plate evinces a mastery of the technique which is unusual. An equally fine example in the Victoria and Albert Museum is regarded as 'probably Venetian' and the technique was certainly being employed elsewhere towards the end of the 16th century.

Opposite, left:
Goblet and cover vertically fluted, the bowl with four gradations of size, Venetian, early 17th century. An outstanding example of the skill of the *vitrearius*.

Opposite, above right:
Cut-glass candelabra, English, *c.* 1770.

Opposite, below:
Oval covered bowl decorated with wheel engraving, Silesian, 18th century.

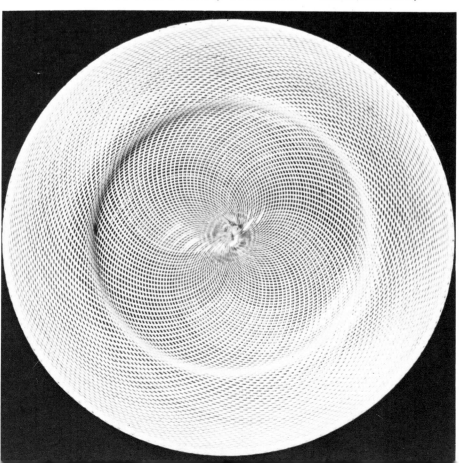

oxides. Unless special precautions have been taken to obviate the defect, glass normally exhibits a slight greenish, yellowish, or bluish tinge caused by impurities in the raw materials, of which iron is the commonest. This unwanted colour can be removed by adding a small quantity of manganese oxide, although too great an amount will colour the glass to a variable shade resembling the appearance of permanganate of potash dissolved in water. Occasionally long exposure to light will cause glass decolourized in this way to develop a faint purplish shade, but this is unusual.

Decolourized glass was termed *cristallo* by the Venetians in the fifteenth century, when they rediscovered this ancient technique, originally known to the Alexandrians in the first century AD. They gave it this name because of its resemblance to the semiprecious hardstone, rock crystal, a quartz that, apart from its crystalline structure, looks very much like glass. Since the fifteenth century clear glass which has little or no adventitious colour has been termed *crystal*, and lead glass has been especially regarded as the finest crystal, probably because, like rock crystal, it was so frequently decorated by engraving and cutting. Rock crystal was worked with abrasive wheels in the same way as other semiprecious hardstones, and a Bohemian hardstone carver, Caspar Lehmann of Prague, working at the end of the sixteenth century, was the first in modern times to use glass in place of rock crystal (page 37). The chandeliers of faceted pendant drops, which were made of glass in the eighteenth and successive centuries, were originally cut from rock crystal. Cameo carving, intaglio cutting, and facet cutting were all derived in the first place from techniques

Glass lends itself to a wide variety of treatments, some of which are shown here.

Above, left:
A Venetian 'winged' goblet at various stages of the manufacture (top) of the bowl, with the complete goblet alongside, and (below, from right to left) of the stem and foot before addition of the bowl. To make the complete glass from its components—foot, stem and bowl—took approximately 2·5 minutes.

Centre, left:
A paperweight with *millefiori* decoration, probably made at Stourbridge, *c.* 1850. There is no documentation for the making of complete weights at Stourbridge, but it is unlikely that so important a glass-making centre would have neglected an item in such great demand.

Centre, right:
A circular plaque of cameo glass engraved by John Woodall, a pupil of John Northwood, Stourbridge, *c.* 1890.

Bottom:
Stages in the making of a *millefiori* paperweight (see page 106).

Opposite, top:
One of a pair of flower holders in crystal glass threaded with ruby, from Stourbridge. Threading of this kind dates from about 1880, when John Northwood invented a machine for making *latticinio* work by drawing coloured threads through molten glass.

Opposite, below:
A vase by Emile Gallé (1845–1905), one of the major influences on the Art Nouveau movement, and one of the earliest. He was much indebted to Japanese art, then the focus of intense interest in France.

Opposite, right:
A Venetian *latticinio* vase enamelled with scattered insects, dating from the late 16th century. *Latticinio* work, so-called from the Italian word for milk, *latte*, is also known as filigree glass—*verre filigraine*, in French.

termed *rose Pompadour*. Kunckel also made artificial rubies from glass coloured in this way.

Silver yields a yellow colour when employed as a colouring agent, but it has rarely been so used. One example is the work of the Bohemian decorator, Anton Kothgasser, early in the nineteenth century. Chromate of lead, introduced during the early decades of the nineteenth century, yields a good yellow, and it replaced the earlier mixture of silver, lead, and antimony which had been used for this purpose. Iron, according to the manner of its use, could be made to yield green, yellow, and a brownish black. For the latter colour it was usually blended with manganese, when a fine dense black could be produced.

All these oxides, except that of tin, could be used to produce a coloured transparent glass, and the colours could be opacified by the addition of tin oxide, which was sometimes employed in the manufacture of the nineteenth-century French glass termed *opaline*. Phosphate of lime procured from calcined ox bones when added to glass produced a semiopaque white glass (the German *Beinglas*) from which opaline was more commonly made, and this also could be coloured with the oxides just mentioned.

The painting of pottery inspired similar decoration on glass. This kind of work came principally from Venice and Germany, and difficulty was at first experienced in firing colours to make them permanent. We find rare specimens from both places decorated in un-fired oil or lacquer colours, the so-called cold colours (German: *Kaltemalerei*—'cold painting'), but enamel colours were developed in Venice in the fifteenth century and in Germany by the middle of the sixteenth century.

Enamel colours are made from finely powdered coloured glass to which a vegetable oil has been added as a medium for painting, as well as a flux to lower the melting point. The colours are applied to the surface of the glass, which is then placed in an enamelling kiln and heated to a point where the powdered glass pigment fuses. At the same time the surface of the glass softens sufficiently for the colours to adhere to it. Although the fusion point of the colours could be lowered by means of a flux to temperatures slightly below that of the glass, in the absence of any accurate methods of measuring temperature great skill and judgement were required in the control of the heat. Early glass colours applied in this way are nearly always opacified with tin oxide, and in contrast to much European enamelling on porcelain which uses an identical technique, the painting is raised in slight relief, because it was too hazardous to allow the glass surface to become soft enough for the colours to sink in. Nevertheless, certain free-lance painters (notably the German *Hausmaler*, or studio painters) achieved a very close approach to the appearance of faïence and porcelain enamelling, and their work is much admired.

employed to carve rock crystal and other hardstones.

There are a number of metallic oxides which have been employed since very early times to add colour to glass. Before the discovery that manganese could be employed to remove the unwanted colour resulting from impurities in the raw materials, glass was frequently coloured, and copper was perhaps the most favoured colouring agent. According to the manner of use copper yields turquoise blue, a shade usually known as copper green, and red. The latter colour develops in a furnace atmosphere which is predominantly of carbon monoxide termed a *reducing* atmosphere, and the product a *reduced colour*. Iron also yields blue, but since the eighteenth century the most popular source of this colour has been cobalt oxide, which is also employed to colour pottery glazes and for underglaze decoration. Opaque white glass results from the addition of tin oxide, and the product is indistinguishable from the pottery glaze covering maiolica or delft. Glass opacified in this way was employed by the Venetians and others to make imitations of porcelain and maiolica. Gold yields a rose colour, and this metal was the basis of the seventeenth-century purple of Cassius, which was employed as a colouring agent by the German glass chemist, Johann Kunckel, at Potsdam, as well as for a pigment for faïence and porcelain painting (e.g., the Chinese *famille rose*), and for the famous porcelain ground colour of Sèvres

The nineteenth century was the age of the chemist, when many new processes were devised and developed, some of which are described later. Generally, however, the principles of glassmaking remained the same, and a number of ancient techniques were revived. Mechanical methods were applied for the first time to glassmaking, and the moulds into which bottles were blown automatically often added decoration in relief of a kind which has made them popular for collections, especially in France and America. Glass pressed into moulds was an American innovation of the early years of the nineteenth century. Press-moulding of this kind can only be used where the opening is at least as wide as the base. The mould is made with the desired pattern in reverse. A measured amount of molten glass is dropped into the heated mould. A plunger, which may bear an interior pattern, is brought down, and squeezes the glass into its final shape, filling the depressions in the mould as it does so. The presses were hand-operated until 1864, when the first steam press was patented. Patterns were diverse and more elaborate than could be achieved by cutting or engraving. The French, especially, produced some excellent reproductions of English cut glass by press-moulding, the best of them the more deceptive because the faceting was in part sharpened on the glass cutter's wheel and any mould seams removed. Similar imitations were made in England, and in the twentieth century mechanization has so speeded

Above :
Opal glass enamelled with
flowers from Stourbridge.
Most 19th-century glass of
this kind falls into two categories—that opacified with
tin oxide, which has the
denseness of the Italian
maiolica pottery glaze, and
the slightly less densely
opaque variety opacified with
calcined cattle bones (lime
phosphate). The former is
usually termed *opal glass,* and
the latter *opaline.* The
enamel colours were fired on
separately at a temperature
lower than the melting point
of the glass, but sufficiently
high to slightly soften its
surface.

Below :
Vase cased with blue and
green over crystal glass and
etched with a landscape
effect, Stourbridge, *c.* 1890.
In its technique this vase
echoes the work of Gallé and
some of his contemporaries.
Casing is the result of dipping
a gathering of glass into
molten glass of another
colour so that it forms the
outer surface of the sub-
sequent object after manipulation. Etched patterns are
formed by protecting part of
the glass with an acid-
resistant varnish, followed by
the application of hydro-
fluoric acid, which attacks the
unprotected part. This is left
in contact with the surface of
the glass until the desired
effect has been achieved.
In modern times use of acid
has to some extent been
superseded by sand blasting.

Far right :
Tazza cased with ruby glass
over opal, with an etched leaf
border and central rosette,
Stourbridge, *c.* 1860. The
tazza, an ornamental dish or
stand on a low foot, with or
without handles, first became
popular in Renaissance Italy,
especially in metalwork,
although examples exist in
glass. The *tazza* is also to be
found made in Georgian
glass towards the end of the
18th century. The form and
motifs of decoration shown
here were popular during the
1850's.

up production that the inferior kinds can be made to be sold for a few pence.

The best moulded imitations of cut glass need careful examination to distinguish them from genuine cut glass of any period. The intricate faceting of cut glass is executed by bringing the surface into contact with rotating wheels charged with abrasive, with only the most summary indications to guide the workman, who depends largely on his eye. Therefore, it is only to be expected that the patterns will not have the mechanical precision and geometrical accuracy of moulded work. The facets of moulded specimens are sometimes sharpened by partial cutting on the wheel, but this is limited to the more obvious areas which are easy to reach. The blunt edges of moulded facets will still be found in the inconspicuous places. The presence of a seam immediately condemns a specimen as moulded, but on the best examples seams are removed by fire polishing. This involves playing the flame of a blowlamp on the surface for long enough to melt it slightly, which not only removes the offending seams, but confers a high polish on the surface. It may, however, have the effect of further blunting the edges of the facets.

Especially during the eighteenth and nineteenth centuries many attempts were made to imitate porcelain in glass. The first efforts were in Venice at the beginning of the sixteenth century, where there is a record of six bowls described as *porcellana contrefacta* (imitation porcelain). These have vanished long since, but were presumably of glass opacified with tin oxide. A little later the Venetians were imitating maiolica with glass printed in cold colour, and in the eighteenth century they produced porcelain plates painted in enamel colours in the manner of contemporary porcelain. White opacified glass was employed in eighteenth-century Germany for the same purpose. It was termed *Milchglas* or, quite commonly, *Porseleinglas*. Both these forms and the painted decoration were as close to those of contemporary porcelain as could be achieved in glass. Similar imitations of porcelain in white glass were made in eighteenth-century England, at Bristol, and contemporary porcelain painting, especially that of Worcester and of China, was copied. These formed fairly distinct and separate categories. Both pottery and porcelain glazes are types of glass.

An interesting category is glass made 'at the lamp'. This is a grouping of small decorative objects made by manipulating glass softened in a flame. The most important examples of this kind are such things as the seventeenth-century glass figures of Nevers, but allied to this work is a group of small decorative pieces, usually fairly crude in workmanship, which are termed *end of day* glass, or *friggers*, and in America *off hand* glass. These were made at the end of the day from the glass remaining in the crucibles, which was the workmen's perquisite. The

forms taken by these small objects are too numerous to record, but walking sticks and hoops of trailed glass may be taken as examples. They were either sold in taverns or given to friends and relatives. The type is almost world-wide in its distribution.

Although glass is a man-made substance, natural glasses also exist. The most widely known is the natural volcanic glass termed *obsidian*. Glass is also sometimes produced when lightning strikes suitable natural materials, and a sea of glass was formed in the Nevada desert when the first atomic bomb was exploded there. Although the usual substances employed to make glass are sand and an alkaline flux, almost any substance containing silica could replace sand, and a flux is principally necessary to lower the melting point to an economic level. It is quite possible to make glass from silica at a temperature of about 1600°C, and this is sometimes done when a special glass is required for scientific purposes.

In the words of an eighteenth-century writer on the subject: 'The Chemists hold that there is no Body but may be *vitrified*, that is, converted into glass . . . and it was a merry saying of a very great Artist in the Business of Glass, that their Profession would be the last in the world, for that when God should consume the Universe with fire, all things therein would be turned to Glass.'

The Art and History of Glass

THE CLASSICAL BEGINNINGS

The origin of the discovery of glass is lost in the mists of antiquity. Pliny tells the story of merchants, encamped on a seashore, who lit a fire underneath a cooking pot supported on lumps of natron (soda), and later found the sand fused into glass. This is certainly fiction, because no campfire could attain the necessary degree of heat.

The first surviving records of glass come from Mesopotamia in the seventeenth century BC, but vitreous glazes had been used in Egypt for covering stone beads and the so-called faïence before 3000 BC. The earliest glasshouse so far discovered is Egyptian, excavated at Tell-el Amarna, and dating from about 1350 BC. The first Egyptian vessels are dated about 1500 BC, and were made by the sand-core method. The core was attached to a metal rod and then either dipped into molten glass or wound round with ductile threads of glass until the desired shape had been obtained. Differently coloured threads were treated in a variety of decorative ways, and were sometimes combed to give a variegated effect.

By the first century BC the manufacture of glass on a large and commercial scale had been established at Sidon, and it is here that glass blowing was probably invented. Glass was an object of trade with the Phoenicians, and the glass of Sidon has been found in many places around the Mediterranean. The Sidon glassmakers may well have been the first to use a trademark by which the glass of particular makers could be identified.

Equally important as a glassmaking centre was the Egyptian port of Alexandria, and Alexandrian glassworkers originated many processes and techniques which were later revived by the Venetians and others. Much glass was exported to Rome from Sidon and Alexandria, and it is often impossible to be sure whether a particular specimen was made in one or other of these two places, or in or around Rome itself. Nevertheless, a glasshouse existed in Rome by 14 AD, and from Rome the art was carried to other parts of the Empire, to Gaul, the Rhineland (where Cologne was an important centre), and probably even England.

The glass of Sidon was, for the most part, a

commercial production, and vessels of domestic utility were made in vast quantities. Decoration, usually mould-blown, is to be found, but a good deal of glass of this kind is plain or slightly ornamented and obviously intended for ordinary domestic use. An excellent example of this is the bottle of square section, which often turns up in excavations, and was in fact manufactured quite widely. It assumed this form because it was more easily packed and took up less room on the shelf.

The more decorative kinds of glassware came from Alexandria, and inherited the earlier Egyptian technical traditions. The distinction between decorative and domestic glass was well marked. Both Alexandria and Rome had well-established schools of hardstone carvers—men who worked on such stones as agate, chalcedony, and especially rock crystal. These were carved with small rotating wheels in conjunction with an abrasive such as emery, and with a diamond point used as a stylus or chisel, and the same techniques were often employed in the making of decorative glass.

In Rome the glassworker who produced glass by blowing, and who ornamented it by often elaborate trailing and related techniques, was termed a *vitrearius*. The glasses made by those who employed the techniques of hardstone carving were termed *diatreta*—especially when in the form of the very rare cage-cups (cups decorated by undercutting in a similar manner to the Lycurgus Cup illustrated on page 23), although the term is often extended to refer to work that involves similar techniques—and the craftsmen themselves were termed *diatretarii*. The similarity of glass to natural hardstones, especially rock crystal, has always been recognized, and many more or less successful attempts have been made to imitate them, especially in Venice and Bohemia, although not all such simulations were decorated by carving.

It is in Rome that we first see a distinct division between the work of the *vitrearius* and the carver, the *diatretarius*, and this division in the craft of glass has persisted to the present day. Perhaps the most spectacular example of the art of the *diatretarius* or cameo cutter is the Portland Vase of the third century AD, although the cage-cup of the Römische-Germanisches Museum (Cologne) and the Lycur-

gus Cup of the British Museum probably excel it technically in the first case, and artistically in the second.

The Portland Vase started as a vase of dark-blue glass cased with white which was blown into a mould, the handles being added afterwards, and to this extent the *vitrearius* participated. It was then given to the cameo cutter who patiently ground away the white layer to form the pattern. It is a technical tour de force which needs careful study to appreciate the skill with which it has been carved. Few have had a better opportunity to study the vase than Josiah Wedgwood, who made the famous jasper copies of it in 1790, and he commented on the way in which the Roman craftsman had cut down towards the blue glass to a point where the darker colour struck faintly through the white to act as shading which enhanced the modelling. This was an effect Wedgwood despaired of achieving in jasper.

In the 1870's John Northwood (1837–1902) of Wordsley, Worcestershire, was commissioned by Benjamin Richardson of Stourbridge to copy the Portland Vase in glass, and seven attempts were necessary before a cased block could be produced for him to work on. In cameo cutting it is essential for the work to be stationary, unlike facet cutting where the abrasive wheels employed are fixed in their position and the work brought to them. Northwood did much of the work with a hammer and hardened steel chisels. Even though he had the advantage of being able to employ hydrofluoric acid to remove some of the unwanted white casing, it took him three years to complete the work, and every day he was faced with the risk that a slip of the tool could ruin his entire labour. Although Northwood trained several pupils, including his son, who also did distinguished work of the same kind, this revival of cameo cutting died out before the end of the century, probably because of the cost of the labour involved.

The history of early glass from almost every production centre is, perforce, a series of deductions from the material that has been preserved, and from written records. It is difficult to conjecture by how much historical surveys are astray, but obviously our knowledge is partial and lacunary, and if an insufficient number of specimens has come down to us, or written records are lacking, then an incomplete and possibly inaccurate picture will follow. For instance, a fourteenth-century Bolognese fresco depicts some technically advanced types of glass, presumably from Venice, none of which have survived.

The Romans became accomplished glassworkers, and much of their common glassware has survived. The more decorative types, which were scarce in the first place, have only rarely been found. Nevertheless, in the field of Roman glass there are specimens, often fragmentary, of almost every process and technique to be found

Above:
The famous Portland Vase, a masterpiece of Roman cameo cutting from the 3rd century AD.

later, although many must have been rediscovered independently by the Venetians and others.

We are most fortunate in having the *Natural History* of Pliny the Elder, because it contains many references to glass. Among them there is information about the almost legendary murrhine vases for which the emperors Caligula and Nero paid large sums. These are sometimes thought to have been a kind of Alexandrian glass, perhaps a *millefiori* type, specimens of which still exist, but this is extremely unlikely. Glass mosaics formed of pieces of coloured glass backed with reflecting metal foil are more brilliant than mosaics of coloured stones. 'Mosaic' glass vessels are those made from sections of coloured glass rod fused together in moulds, a process which was the precursor of the later *millefiori* technique, and which came originally from Alexandria.

The art of colouring glass was learned from the Alexandrians, and Pliny refers to a large number of colours and shades, including *haematinum*, a lead glass which was blood red in shade—a reduced copper colour (see page 16). The highest value, however, was placed upon clear, transparent glass resembling rock crystal, in which the glass had been decolourized with manganese, using a technique first developed in Alexandria.

Pliny refers to statues of glass, about which nothing is definitely known, but these were probably made from blocks of cast glass shaped or finished with chisels and abrasives. Glass vessels and decorative objects have certainly been made in this way from solid cast blocks,

Below:
Mosaic glass bowl, the forerunner of later *millefiori* glass, Alexandria, late 3rd century AD. This type of glass is sometimes thought to be the murrhine glass prized by the Romans, but this is doubtful.

used as though they were blocks of rock crystal, by Islamic and Chinese glassworkers, although such objects are only of small size.

Wheel engraving with simple patterns is found on Syrian glass of an early date, and Roman glass was also decorated in this way, although specimens of such work are rare. Facet cutting first occurred later in the first century AD, and diamond-point engraving was practised, although very few examples of it have survived.

Glass enamelling was a Roman innovation. Specimens are in the treasury of St Mark's, Venice, and the Römische-Germanisches Museum, Cologne. Cold painting was employed to decorate glass, and may have been used extensively, but few specimens are now known because decoration of this kind is extremely vulnerable, and rarely survives burial.

'Gold sandwich' glass, which may have originated either in Palestine or Alexandria, was certainly made in Rome, though it may have been a late introduction. This technique required the manufacture of two glass vessels, one fitting precisely inside the other. The exterior of the inner vessel was covered with gold leaf, which was scraped away in part to form patterns. The two vessels were then put together and the edge sealed. This is basically the technique of the eighteenth-century German *Zwischengoldgläser.*

Roman window glass was cast on a flat bed and was therefore a kind of plate glass, but even though the sheets were of comparatively large size, they were also half an inch thick and translucent rather than transparent. Pliny mentions

glass mirrors, which seem to have come from Sidon, but nothing of this nature has survived, and his descriptions are so obscure that it is difficult to be sure of his meaning. It would be impossible to make an efficient mirror from plate glass half an inch thick, but in the fourteenth century convex mirrors were being made in Lorraine by cutting curved segments from a blown sphere, and it is quite possible that mirrors of this kind were known to the Romans.

Much, perhaps most, ancient glass has been found in excavations, and burial eventually decomposes glass. The process of decomposition begins on the surface with the formation of an iridescence. This is a colourful layer which is often somewhat analogous to the corroded patination of old bronze, but usually, however, it is little more than a rainbow-like display of colour on the immediate surface. The latter kind of iridescence in particular has attracted the attention of such later glassmakers as Lötz Witwe of Klostermühle in Austria and Louis Tiffany of New York. Reproductions of old Roman glass have been given a fairly deceptive iridescence by immersing them for a few months in a cesspit, but the glass itself rarely backs up the deception.

The fall of the Roman Empire also meant temporary victory for the *vitrearius,* no doubt because, with the parallel collapse of the monetary system, few people were left able to pay for more elaborate and time-consuming work. Decorative glass did not reappear in Europe until the revival of commerce which accompanied the flourishing of the Florentine Renaissance early in the fourteenth century.

Above, left :
Syrian glass bottle exhibiting iridescence, *c.* 1st century AD. Glass is affected in this way after long contact with water and carbonic acid gas, conditions inseparable from burial in damp soil containing humus. Iridescence is analogous to the corrosion found in excavated bronze, and both often have an attractive coloration prized by collectors.

Centre, left :
The Lycurgus Cup, by transmitted light. The glass contains a minute quantity of colloidal gold (i.e., gold in particles too small to sink in a suspensory liquid) which is probably responsible for the colour when the cup is held up to the light. The effect is not uncommon and occurs in certain later glasses.

Bottom :
Model of a 14th- or 15th-century English glasshouse, set in a forest clearing, and probably also typical of the *Waldglashütten* of Central Europe. English glasshouses of this kind were mostly located in Sussex, a prolific source of charcoal.

Right :
Vase with iridized surface by Lötz Witwe, Austria, *c.* 1880. Deliberately iridized glass, apparently inspired by excavated Roman or Syrian glass, was introduced by the Viennese firm of Lobmeyr in the 1870's. It was quickly taken up by Witwe and at Stourbridge, and later by Tiffany, Carder and others.

GLASS IN THE MEDIEVAL PERIOD

In the interval, often termed the Dark Ages, domestic glass was made in the forests, the so-called *Waldglas*. Page 26 shows a reconstruction of an English glasshouse that made this type of glass. *Waldglas*, unless made with imported soda—which rarely happened—was a potash glass, fluxed with the ashes of ferns and other forest plants. Nevertheless, it was not until much later than the product acquired the characteristics we now associate with potash glass as made in Bohemia, and its manufacture was originally limited to blown glass, often with trailed decoration. The standard of craftsmanship was high save in exceptional cases, although many such objects have come to have considerable aesthetic and antiquarian value. The makers of *Waldglas* had discovered the advantages of adding lime in larger quantities than was normally present in the ash they used. It made glass more durable, stronger, and less likely to deteriorate when in prolonged contact with water.

Frankish glass, a type widely distributed across Europe, was principally made in Belgium between the fifth and eighth centuries AD. It was an article of trade, but the type was also made in several countries, perhaps including England. The most typical Frankish glasses, although specimens of them are among the rarest, are the drinking horn made in the shape of earlier oxhorn drinking cups, and the claw beaker (*Rüsselbecher*), which is a very rare form of beaker with drawn-out hollow projections that curve downwards and rejoin the surface at a lower point. Other Frankish glasses exhibit the influence of the Roman *vitrearius*.

By the early ninth century the art of glass-making had almost disappeared. The only written materials on the subject to survive at that date were Pliny's chapters in his *Natural History*, but these, despite their valuable information on the place of glass in Roman society, hardly provided reliable technical assistance. A ninth-century compilation made by a monk named Theophilus gave more practical information, but in fact drew heavily on Roman sources including Pliny. To the Church the making of glass was a kind of black magic and consequently discouraged, especially for such church furniture as chalices.

The production of glass continued in several places in the East, notably in Syria and in Egypt, and when the conquests of the followers of Mohammed began in the eighth century, these centres one by one fell into their hands, together with libraries of books dating back to Imperial Roman times. The making of glass was encouraged by the Mohammedans, who made a point of preserving and consulting many of the Roman manuscripts, which unfortunately have since been lost.

It is very difficult to determine the provenance, or the date, of much of the earliest

Left, above:
Beaker of amber glass made in a three-piece mould, Syrian, second half of 1st century AD. An excavated specimen with some iridescence, this is an excellent example of moulded glass of the period.

Left, below:
Claw beaker of green glass with blue trailing, found at Castle Eden, Co. Durham, in 1775, late 5th/early 6th century AD. Blobs of softened glass were applied to the surface and then drawn out with pincers. Of all the decorative techniques known to the Romans the early *Waldglas* makers seem only to have retained the use of trailing. The claw is a development of a type of ornament first used by the Roman *vitrearius*, but carried to much greater lengths. The claw beakers are perhaps the finest things to survive from what has been aptly called the Dark Ages, principally because so little is known about the period.

Opposite, above:
Cone beaker of olive-green glass with trailed decoration from Gotland, Sweden, 7th century AD. The shape of this beaker testifies to the drinking habits of the owner, because once it was filled, he could not have put it down unemptied.

Opposite, below:
Beaker decorated with relief cutting, the so-called Hedwig type, Islamic glass, 12th century AD. This very rare glass was no doubt made by a lapidary accustomed to working with rock crystal. Examples exist of vessels cut from a solid block of glass, which are obviously the work of a rock-crystal cutter, who always began with a block of this kind.

Bottom:
Drinking horn of amber glass found in Germany, 5th century AD. The cow's horn must have been the earliest drinking vessel, still in use when this glass version was made. It is impossible to do more than guess where most of these glasses might have been made.

Islamic glass, but two sources of excavated specimens (usually fragmentary) are Samarra on the Tigris (especially the site of the palace of the Abbasid Caliph Mu'tasim), and the rubbish heaps of Fostat (Old Cairo) in Egypt. Samarra was occupied between 836 and 883 AD, so specimens can be dated fairly closely as not later than 883 AD. Excavations here have brought to light examples of many techniques known to the Romans, and later employed in Europe almost up to the present day. Many fragments of glass cut in the manner of rock crystal have been found. Perhaps the most important of surviving specimens of work of this kind are the cameo-cut glasses of twelfth-century Egyptian workmanship, termed *Hedwig* glasses, most of which are preserved in the Schlesisches Museum in Breslau. They are so called because there is a tradition that they once belonged to St Hedwig, who died in 1243.

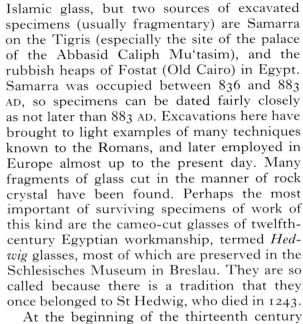

At the beginning of the thirteenth century the Islamic glassworkers of Syria and Mesopotamia had mastered the art of enamelling and gilding glass, and were employing the metallic lustre pigments which the potters of the region had been using since the ninth century. The best-known examples of Islamic enamelled glass are mosque lamps, which usually come from Syria. Specimens of this kind of glass were also brought back from the East by the European Crusaders, and some of these, like the 'Luck of Edenhall' (page 30), have survived.

Byzantine glass is represented in one or two of the more important collections by a few doubtfully attributed specimens, mostly fragmentary. It is probable that a technically well-advanced glass industry existed in Byzantium in the thirteenth century, but this assertion is based on written records rather than on surviving examples.

Theophilus, for instance, who compiled his *De Diversis Artibus* at the beginning of the twelfth century, describes the making of enamelled glass by Byzantine workmen, and his description of painting in colours leaves little doubt of the nature of the process. He refers also to the making of goblets of purple or blue glass with handles of white glass and trailed white glass ornamentation.

VENETIAN GLASS

Venice, at the head of the Adriatic, was a city which had traditionally traded with both Byzantium and the cities of the Near East. Despite papal attempts to proscribe trading with the Saracens, Venetian contacts with the Near East continued, even during the Crusades, and there is little doubt that the sack of Byzantium by the Crusaders in 1204 was a diversion planned by the then Doge, Enrico Dandolo, to prevent the Christian troops from attacking the Sultan of Egypt, who was one of Venice's best customers. Some of the best of the Byzantine craftsmen migrated to Venice, and another such influx took place in 1402, from Syria, after Tamerlane and his Mongol invaders had captured Damascus. The exotic cargoes which were shipped into Venice included glass from Damascus and Aleppo, and from Alexandria in Egypt. It is also probable that Venetians went to the Near East to learn the craft of glassmaking there.

Although glassmaking had been carried on in Venice since early times the industry only became firmly established after 1204. Its development, however, was rapid, and a guild of glassworkers was in existence by 1224, although no reliably attributed specimen of its work survives which can be dated before the middle of the fifteenth century. By 1291 the industry was on so large a scale that the danger of the furnaces setting fire to the city became too great, and the Senate decreed their removal to the island of Murano, where they have remained to this day.

The first glasses which can undeniably be attributed to Venice are some silver-pattern

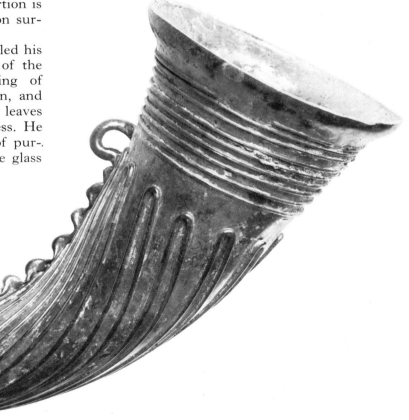

Above, left:
Milchglas beaker painted with
a village scene in the manner
of porcelain, Venice, *c.* 1740,
marked *Al Gésu*. Al Gésu was
a glasshouse at Murano
belonging to the Miotti
family which existed from
the early 17th century.
Several examples thus marked
are known, dated between
1731 and 1747. A factory for
the manufacture of porcelain
in the manner of Meissen was
established in Venice by the
brothers Vezzi in 1730. Porcelain generally was extremely
fashionable and made con-
siderable inroads into markets
formerly supplied by the
manufacturers of glass. So it is
not surprising that Venetian
glassmakers should attempt
to make an imitation
porcelain.

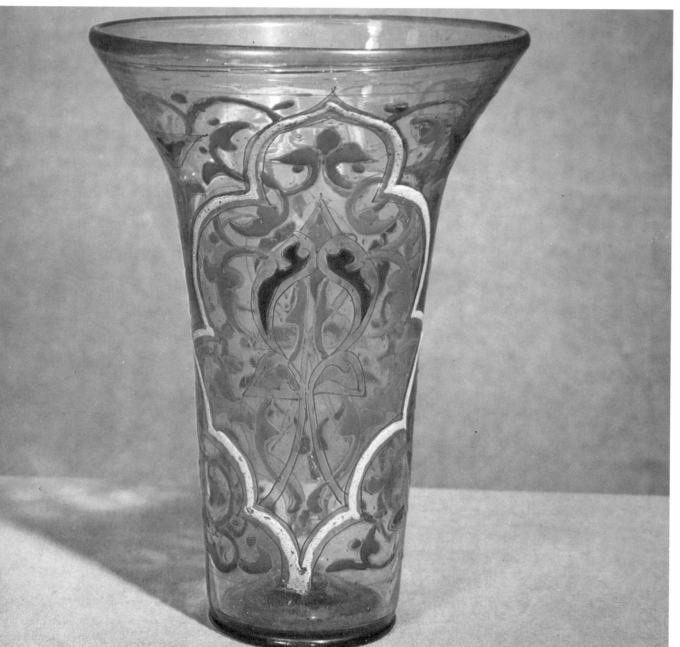

Below, left:
'The Luck of Edenhall',
Islamic enamelled glass,
second half of the 13th
century. It is accompanied by
an English 14th-century cut-
leather case, so it has been in
England at least since that
date, perhaps brought back by
a returning Crusader, to
whom it would have been a
precious rarity. Glass of this
kind was also imported from
Islamic sources by the
Venetians and exported to
Northern Europe.

Opposite:
Miniature ewer of *millefiori*
glass with silver-gilt mounts,
Venice, 16th century. The
technique employed was
inspired by the mosaic
glass of Alexandria, but it
differs from that of the
Alexandrians because the
cane sections are embedded
in clear glass instead of being
arranged side by side in a
mould and fused together.
Mounting in precious metals
was employed during the 16th
century particularly for
highly valued objects. The
rare specimens of Chinese
porcelain to reach Europe
were often mounted in this
way.

Above:
Beaker enamelled with a coat of arms, Venice, early 16th century. Although enamelling as a decorative technique became unfashionable in Venice by 1530, glasses enamelled with armorial devices, principally those of German and Bohemian noblemen, were made for export for perhaps another 50 years. Tradition has it that the town of Bardějov (Czechoslovakia) ordered six such goblets in 1500, both for official use and as models for the glasshouse nearby. Five of them still exist and are in the town museum.

Below, left:
Covered beaker of wheel-engraved ruby glass mounted at Augsburg in silver-gilt, last quarter of the 17th century. Ruby glass was at one time thought to be the discovery of Johann Kunckel (1630–1703), who published his *Ars Vitraria Experimentalis* in 1679, but the colouring agent he employed —gold chloride—was discovered by Andreas Cassius of Leiden, probably before 1679.

Below, right:
Vase of opaque white glass in the form of a pecten or scallop shell, Venice, last quarter of the 16th century. The shell of the *pecten jacobæus* was an emblem of St James, patron saint of Spain, borne by pilgrims who had visited his shrine at Compostella. The saint is also symbolized by a pilgrim bottle on a staff. The shell itself was a common ornamental motif in European decorative art and can be found carved on the knees of the cabriole legs of 18th-century English chairs.

Opposite:
Reichsadlerhumpen (Imperial eagle beaker), Bohemia, dated 1599. This is a variation of the more usual type, by which the Crucifixion has been superimposed on the double-headed eagle of the Holy Roman Empire. The decoration is in opaque enamels on a brownish glass. Opaque colours are typical of German enamelling of the period. An earlier specimen of this *humpen*, dated 1571, is in the British Museum.

goblets, late Gothic in form, which date from the second half of the fifteenth century. These were enamelled with a variety of subjects taken from illuminated manuscripts. The colour of the glass is usually deep blue, but a few are green, even fewer turquoise, and a white example is in the Narodny Museum in Prague. A particularly well-known example of the group is the Victoria and Albert Museum's Fairfax Cup which is turquoise blue from the addition of copper oxide. This colouring agent yields either turquoise blue or red according to the furnace atmosphere, which, when there is an excess of carbon monoxide, produces copper-red, often termed a transmutation colour. Like other turquoise-blue objects made out of glass, the Fairfax Cup appears red when held up to the light.

The Prague white goblet was opacified with tin oxide, a substance already in use in the making of the opaque white glass which forms the glaze of the kind of Italian pottery termed maiolica. By the early years of the sixteenth century the glassworkers of Venice were attempting to provide substitutes for both maiolica and Chinese porcelain, the latter a rare and valued import into Venice from the East.

The six bowls of *porcellana contrefacta* mentioned in the previous chapter have long

since disappeared, and there is no further record of this kind of work until the eighteenth century, when Venetian glassworkers began imitating plates of the newly discovered European porcelain in enamelled white glass, known as *lattimo*. The eighteenth century saw similar imitations made in Germany, where this opaque white glass was termed *Milchglas* or *Porseleinglas*.

Venetian imitations of maiolica were painted with cold colour on the underside of clear glass plates, and the painting was varnished afterwards as a protection. The subjects were either copied directly from maiolica, or taken from the sources used by the maiolica potters, such as the popular prints after Raphael by Marcantonio Raimondi. The more elaborately decorated maiolica plates were intended not for domestic use but to be displayed on buffets, and Venetian glass plates of this kind were undoubtedly employed for the same purpose.

The discovery that unwanted colour in clear glass could be neutralized by adding a small quantity of manganese oxide had originally been made by the Alexandrians, and the fact was rediscovered by the Venetians before 1500. By the early years of the sixteenth century a reasonably colourless glass was being produced and termed *cristallo* from its resemblance to rock crystal. Colourless glass of good quality has been termed *crystal* ever since. A little before 1500 the Venetians began to enamel colourless glass, and by the sixteenth century they were supplying their Islamic customers with glass of this kind to special order. There is, for example, a record of orders for mosque lamps that dates from about this time, presumably of the thirteenth-century type originally made in Syria and intended to be suspended from the mosque ceiling by chains (page 95). The production of these in Syria had ceased with Tamerlane's capture of Damascus in 1402. By 1530, however, enamelling had fallen out of favour in Venice except for export orders to Germany, where the type inspired a whole category of glasses which went on being manufactured in Bohemia, Silesia, and elsewhere in the Holy Roman Empire till well into the eighteenth century.

Enamelling and cold painting are both akin in their decorative effect to enamelling on pottery and metal, and the glass itself serves largely as a support for the painting rather than being something decorative in its own right. With the discovery of *cristallo* glass, and the decline of enamelling, the Venetians began to develop the plastic potentialities of soda glass, carrying them to lengths never approached before or since. The craft of the *vitrearius* had been brought to its utmost limits in complexity.

Soda glass, especially that of Venice which was thin, almost horny in appearance, is unsuitable for either wheel engraving or facet cutting, but a certain amount of diamond engraving was undertaken, and by the last quarter of the sixteenth century this technique

had been brought to London by an *émigré* Muranese glassmaker named Giacomo Verzelini. By 1534 it had reached Hall-in-the-Tirol, where an important glasshouse under the patronage of the Archduke Ferdinand produced a good deal of excellent glass decorated in this fashion.

In Venice itself the glassworkers principally turned their attention to exploiting the plasticity of their material. Increasingly, goblets and *bouquetières* (flower vases) were provided with elaborate stems built up from trailed glass, often of more than one colour and usually with pincered ornament in addition, the most complex of which are often referred to as 'winged' goblets (page 57). The amazing dexterity of the Venetian *vitrearii* was occasionally approached by glassworkers elsewhere. These men were either *émigrés* from Venice or their pupils, and their work, in common with other types of glass originating elsewhere but based on Venetian techniques and styles, is usually described as *façon de Venise*. The ingenuity of the *vitrearius* may be observed in the employment of threads of *lattimo* (opaque white) glass to make elaborate patterns embedded in clear glass, called *latticinio*, the more intricate patterns being termed *vitro di trina* (lace glass), or *vitro a reticelli*.

Excavations of Roman remains were being carried on in the fifteenth and sixteenth centuries and it is not improbable that these and related techniques were suggested to the Venetians by discoveries of Roman glass. The revival must have taken place before 1540, because in this year Biringuccio referred to vessels made of white or other coloured glass 'which seemed as if woven of twigs placed with great equality and correctness of bounds'. An inventory made in 1542 for Henry VIII also refers to glasses of this type.

Allied to work of this kind is the use of sections of coloured canes in the *millefiori* technique. In Venice this seems to date from the sixteenth century, although it was known in the fifteenth. In 1495 the librarian of St Mark's, Marcantonio Sabellico, wrote of the inclusion of 'all sorts of flowers, such as clothe the meadows in spring, in a little ball', which sounds remarkably like the *millefiori* paperweights of the nineteenth century. Although Venetian work of this sort is rare, it continued until the eighteenth century and was revived in the nineteenth.

An early Venetian development was a glass called *calcedonio*. This imitated a number of the semiprecious hardstones, and was probably inspired by Alexandrian work. An inventory of the duc de Berry of 1416 refers to glass that imitates agate, but no specimen of this date is known from Venice. A treatise of 1443 exists which gives directions for making glass of this kind. Most early glasses imitate agate or jasper, and some rare glasses simulate lapis lazuli, while in the eighteenth century Venetian glass-

makers produced a glass that imitated the brownish quartz with gold-coloured spangles known as aventurine by mixing specks of copper with glass of the requisite colour. A speciality of the Miotti glasshouse, its name, *avventurino*, implies that it was a chance discovery.

Although workers migrated from Venice to other parts of Europe, the Republic went to great lengths to prevent them from going, or to bring them back if they escaped the vigilance of the authorities. Even in the eighteenth century the statutes which decreed assassination as the ultimate sanction had not disappeared from the Venetian legal code. As a trading port with the East, Venice had a rival in Genoa, not far from which was an important centre of glassmaking at Altare. Over the years a number of Venetian workmen escaped to Altare, whose glass industry had been in existence since the tenth century, and was in a particularly flourishing condition in the fifteenth. This was a time when Venice suffered a period of financial stringency following the Turkish capture of Byzantium in 1453, and its trading activities received a further serious check from the discovery of the Cape route to the Far East by the Portuguese in 1486. The Venetian merchants never entirely recovered from this and Lisbon replaced Venice as the centre of Far Eastern trade. The essential difference between the glass industries of Venice and Altare is that the latter actually encouraged workmen to migrate to Northern Europe, and they took the secrets of manufacture with them. Contemporary records refer to glass made in the styles of Venice and Altare as '*façon de Venise*' and '*façon d'Altare*', but surviving records of the glass made at Altare are very scanty, its products can rarely be identified with certainty, and it is difficult to distinguish the two types. Glass made *façon d'Altare* came from France, Germany, Spain, and the Netherlands.

GERMAN GLASS

Reference has been made to the export of enamelled glass from Venice to the German territories in the first half of the sixteenth century. At this time what is now East and West Germany and Czechoslovakia was a group of territories under the suzerainty of the Holy Roman Emperor, who was elected by the principal subsidiary rulers termed *Kurfürsten*, or Electors, sometimes written *Churfürst* in the sixteenth and seventeenth centuries. These at first numbered seven, and comprised three secular princes—the Count-Palatine of the Rhineland, the Duke of Saxony, and the Markgraf of Brandenburg; three spiritual electors—the Archbishops of Mainz, Trèves, and Cologne; to which was added the King of Bohemia. Bavaria was added to the Electorate in 1623, and Hanover in 1710. After the Elector of Hanover became George I of England, the title remained with English sovereigns till 1873.

33

Above:
Beaker enamelled with a coat of arms, Venice, early 16th century. Although enamelling as a decorative technique became unfashionable in Venice by 1530, glasses enamelled with armorial devices, principally those of German and Bohemian noblemen, were made for export for perhaps another 50 years. Tradition has it that the town of Bardějov (Czechoslovakia) ordered six such goblets in 1500, both for official use and as models for the glasshouse nearby. Five of them still exist and are in the town museum.

Below, left:
Covered beaker of wheel-engraved ruby glass mounted at Augsburg in silver-gilt, last quarter of the 17th century. Ruby glass was at one time thought to be the discovery of Johann Kunckel (1630–1703), who published his *Ars Vitraria Experimentalis* in 1679, but the colouring agent he employed —gold chloride—was discovered by Andreas Cassius of Leiden, probably before 1679.

Below, right:
Vase of opaque white glass in the form of a pecten or scallop shell, Venice, last quarter of the 16th century. The shell of the *pecten jacobæus* was an emblem of St James, patron saint of Spain, borne by pilgrims who had visited his shrine at Compostella. The saint is also symbolized by a pilgrim bottle on a staff. The shell itself was a common ornamental motif in European decorative art and can be found carved on the knees of the cabriole legs of 18th-century English chairs.

Opposite:
Reichsadlerhumpen (Imperial eagle beaker), Bohemia, dated 1599. This is a variation of the more usual type, by which the Crucifixion has been superimposed on the double-headed eagle of the Holy Roman Empire. The decoration is in opaque enamels on a brownish glass. Opaque colours are typical of German enamelling of the period. An earlier specimen of this *humpen*, dated 1571, is in the British Museum.

This brief account is desirable because the nature of the Electorate is not always well understood outside Germany, and the arms of the Electors occur on a notable group of enamelled drinking glasses known as *Kurfürstenhumpen*. It also serves to explain the appearance of engraved portraits of English Hanoverian Kings on eighteenth-century German glasses.

The earliest native German enamelling occurs on glass which is almost indistinguishable from *Waldglas*, or forest glass, which was made in small, primitive, glasshouses (*Waldglashütten*) sited in the forests, the source of the potash flux, and moved from place to place as the immediately available fuel became exhausted. The early products of these glass-houses were generally primitive, and the glassware was coloured faintly green by impurities in the source of silica. Such glasses are an uncommon survival, and range in date from the fourteenth century to the sixteenth. Obvious descendants from the Frankish glasses of medieval times, some of them are decorated in a manner reminiscent of the claw beakers, especially the *Krautstrunk* (cabbage-stalk glass), the *Warzenbecher* (wart or nipple beakers), and the *Igel*, or hedgehog beaker.

The glasses imported into Germany from Venice in the first half of the sixteenth century were painted with arms, and early specimens from the German territories were also decorated with armorial bearings. Among the earliest German enamelled glasses are the cylindrical beakers termed *Stangengläser* (pole glasses), so called from their long and slender shapes. The British Museum possesses two such glasses with the arms and portraits of Jacob Praun of Nürnberg and his wife (see left). Sometimes thought to be Venetian glass enamelled in Germany, they are dated about 1589. Earlier specimens of this category are known. The most impressive are the *Reichsadlerhumpen* (Imperial eagle tankard), a type of large cylindrical covered beaker, and the earliest known specimen, in the British Museum, is dated 1571. The double-headed eagle is the coat of arms of the Holy Roman Emperor, and on either side are the arms of the secular and spiritual Electors. Below the arms of the Electors are those of the various minor social categories whose territories comprised the Empire arranged according to the Quaternion system (page 35). The glass painters seem to have used a print made in 1511 for many glasses of this kind. Specimens bear dates from 1571 almost to the end of the seventeenth century, but some quite deceptive reproductions were made by the Fleischmann Company of Nürnberg in the nineteenth century.

The *Kurfürstenhumpen* are a group of cylindrical beakers like the *Reichsadlerhumpen*, which bear the arms of the Electors, and sometimes their portraits also. The *Hofkellereigläser* (court cellar glasses), dating from 1610, are, as the name suggests, goblets made for court use. They bear the arms of the nobleman for whom they were made, and most such glasses still in existence come from Saxony. The *Willkom* glass bears an inscription to welcome guests, and the *Hallorengläser*, painted with a procession of the saltworkers of Halle-an-der-Saale, were made expressly for the workers, the earliest recorded being dated 1679. The *Apostelgläser* depict the Twelve Apostles, and are among the few types with a religious connotation; commemorative glasses are much more common, as are those bearing guild symbols, allegorial subjects, and (not unusual) coarsely erotic painting.

Enamelled glasses of this kind were made in Bohemia, Silesia, Franconia, Thuringia, Saxony, Hesse, Brunswick and Brandenburg. They are not always easy to assign to particular districts, but coats of arms are sometimes helpful, the Saxon arms on some *Hofkellerei* glasses, for instance, being evidence of their manufacture in Saxony. Assignable to Franconia are the *Ochsenkopf* (Oxhead) glasses, so called because they depict a mountain of that name in the Fichtelgebirge area in conjunction with an oxhead. Bohemian enamels are frequently of brighter and better quality than those from elsewhere.

Even the best of the enamelled glasses of this type are inclined to be primitive and naive in execution, but in this second half of the seventeenth century a novel type of glass painting made its appearance, executed by painters in studios and fired in their own kilns instead of on the premises where the glasses were made. These men also painted white faïence in the same way. Painting of this kind is termed *Hausmalerei* (literally, home painting), and the work of the *Hausmäler* is much sought after. In the eighteenth century such painters turned to work in porcelain, to the neglect of glass and faïence, but the rise in popularity of porcelain in Germany provoked its imitation in *Milchglas*, suitably painted. This was produced principally in Bohemia and at a small glasshouse in Basdorf, near Potsdam, which was in operation during the 1750's.

Enamelled glasses are primarily the work of the *vitrearius*, but potash glass is exceptionally well suited to wheel engraving and facet cutting. The most important aspect of German glass in the sixteenth and seventeenth centuries is the return to the scene of the *diatretarius*. Excellent diamond engraving had been done at Hall-in-the-Tirol since about 1534, and the Victoria and Albert Museum has a *Humpen* engraved with a portrait of Emperor Rudolf II and the Electors dated 1594, which may perhaps have been taken from the same original as an enamelled version of the subject which is dated 1592.

Working in Prague for Rudolf II was Caspar Lehmann (1570?–1622), an engraver of rock crystal who turned his attention to glass, and a rare specimen of his work is illustrated opposite.

Opposite:
Pair of *Stangengläser* (pole glasses) enamelled with portraits of Jacob Praun and his wife Clara, with their respective coats of arms, *c.* 1589. The attribution of these glasses is uncertain. They are probably German, but may have been made in Venice.

Below:
Hofkellereiglas (court cellar glass) decorated with the arms of Johann Georg, Elector of Saxony, in coloured enamels, Saxony, 1677.

Right, above:
Panel with engraved portrait of Christian II, Elector of Saxony, made by the lapidary Caspar Lehmann in 1606. Lehmann was the master engraver of his period.

Far right:
Covered box of rock crystal (*Bergkristal*) engraved with a landscape by Georg Schwanhardt of Nürnberg, first half of the 17th century. Schwanhardt was Lehmann's pupil, but this work of his is included primarily for comparison of the medium of rock crystal with that of glass.

Right:
Wheel-engraved Williamite glass, *c.* 1745. These glasses relating to William III, the Dutch husband of James II's daughter Mary, were made for the anti-Jacobite faction which opposed the claim to the throne of James's son and grandson in the 18th century.

Rudolf granted Lehmann a privilege (or monopoly) for this kind of work which, on his death, passed to his pupil, Georg Schwanhardt of Nürnberg (1601–57). Several signed examples of Schwanhardt's work still exist and one, in rock crystal, is shown here. He employed a mixture of wheel and diamond engraving, and exhibits both matt and polished surfaces. His sons, Georg and Heinrich, continued their father's work, and it is probable that Heinrich discovered hydrofluoric acid accidentally but failed to isolate it. A partially etched glass by his hand, dated 1686, is in the Germanisches Museum, Nürnberg, but the acid itself remained undiscovered till 1770.

Towards the end of the seventeenth century a glasshouse under the patronage of the Elector of Brandenburg was set up in Potsdam under the direction of Johann Kunckel. In 1679 Kunckel published a treatise entitled *Ars Vitraria Experimentalis*, based on the *Arte Vetraria* of 1612, by the Venetian Antonio Neri. The earliest Potsdam glass suffered from a defect known as *crisseling* (see page 49), and Kunckel overcame this by including chalk (lime carbonate) in his glass. Especially noteworthy however, was Kunckel's discovery of a way of using the purple of Cassius, a colour which varies from rose pink to purple and is especially employed in pottery and porcelain decoration, to make a ruby-coloured glass. He made glass of several other colours, as well as imitations of semi-precious stones, and the opaque white glass (*Milchglas*) which, appropriately painted, later became known as *Porseleinglas*.

The influence of rock crystal should not be underestimated. Not only did it inspire the development of seventeenth-century cameo cutting (*Hochschnitt*) and intaglio cutting (*Tiefschnitt*), but chandeliers with pendent, facet-cut ornament were originally made from rock crystal, and only later from glass. The Galerie des Glaces at Versailles was illuminated by chandeliers of this kind. Towards the end of the seventeenth century distinguished *Hochschnitt* (high relief) work was being done by Friedrich Winter at Petersdorff on heavy glasses in the form of the *Pokal*, a large covered goblet inspired by silversmiths' work. Winter's brother, Martin, worked at Potsdam in Johann Kunckel's glasshouse, where he was assisted by his cousin, Gottfried Spiller, who was also a master of intaglio engraving. Distinguished work was done by other engravers at

Above:
Humpen (beaker) decorated in *Schwarzlot*, *Hausmalerei* by Hermann Benckertt (*fl.* 1670–80), Nürnberg, 1691. *Schwarzlot* is the name given to painting predominantly in black enamel, a technique introduced by Johann Schaper (1621–70) of Nürnberg, of whom Benckertt was a pupil. When the decoration, as in this case, is predominantly linear it is probably copied from engravings. *Hausmalerei* (painting executed in private workshops) was limited in the 17th century to Germany and Bohemia and specimens are rare.

Below:
Pair of glass figures in the manner of porcelain, Nevers, France, 18th century. Figures made of glass softened 'at the lamp' and manipulated into shape are first recorded as coming from Nevers in 1605, when Louis XIII collected such work. Some of the glass workers later migrated to Paris, where Pierre La Motte enjoyed the patronage of Louis XIV.

Opposite:
Cántaro with *latticinio* decoration, Spanish, 18th century. The Spanish glass industry developed under Venetian influence in the 16th century and although the *cántaro* is essentially a Spanish form, it also occurs in Venetian glass, perhaps made for export to Spain.

Potsdam, but the glasshouse was removed to Zechlin in 1736, and by 1760 glass engraving had been discontinued. One of the most important seventeenth-century glass engravers, Franz Gondelach, was *Hofglasschneider* (court glass cutter) to the Landgraf of Hessen-Cassel. Surviving work from his hand is rare. There were also glass-engraving and hardstone-cutting mills at Dresden, staffed by Bohemian engravers, which were part of the porcelain and artificial hardstone researches of Walther von Tschirnhaus, who had the encouragement of the Elector, August der Starke.

The diamond engraving done in the first half of the sixteenth century at Hall-in-the-Tirol, was executed on glass of several colours, but principally on colourless glass of the type the Venetians termed cristallo. In Germany Georg Schwanhardt the Elder employed this technique in conjunction with wheel engraving.

GLASS IN THE NETHERLANDS AND THE RHINELAND

The seventeenth century also saw the development of diamond engraving in the Netherlands, where it became almost a speciality. The best known of these early engravers was Anna Roemers Visscher (1583–1651) from whose hand several dated specimens have survived. Her sister, Maria Tesselschade (1594–1649), and another woman, Maria von Schurmann (1607–78), did work in a similar style. Willem Jacobz van Heemskerk (1615–92) of Leiden has left several signed glasses of this kind.

Anna Roemers Visscher's glasses were engraved with designs of fruit and flowers which she took from contemporary prints, and encircling borders and inscriptions in the Greek and Latin alphabets done in a linear style, with cross-hatching where required. One glass exists which proves that she was perhaps the first to employ the stippling technique, as well as diamond engraving. This may possibly have been suggested by the new technique of the mezzotint, invented by Ludwig von Siegen in 1643, but a more likely source of inspiration is goldsmiths' work, in which linear engraving was employed in conjunction with the dotting punch. However, Aert Schumann (1720–92), a later Dutch practitioner of the art, also engraved mezzotints, and both diamond and stipple engravings were often based on contemporary prints.

Glass stippling was executed with a diamond point in a holder which was held against the surface of the glass and struck with a light hammer, leaving behind a shallow dot. From these dots, which could be widely or closely spaced according to the demands of the pattern, the picture was built up. Stipple engraving was brought to the point of being an art in itself and not a mere adjunct to line engraving, by Frans Greenwood (1680–1761), who worked in Holland. His work was likened by a contem-

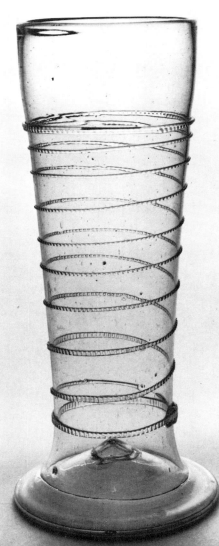

Above :
Blue glass vase decorated with
exotic birds in gold in the
manner of contemporary
porcelain, Bristol glass,
c. 1765. Exotic birds of this
kind were first employed on
Rococo porcelain decorated
at the French royal factory of
Sèvres. This vase may have
been painted by James Giles
of Clerkenwell, an English
Hausmaler, who painted
porcelain bought 'in white'
from Chelsea, Bow,
Worcester and elsewhere.
The decoration of this vase
closely resembles that of
certain Chelsea vases of
c. 1763 which can reasonably be
attributed to Giles's studio.

Below :
Model of an 18th-century
English crystal glass cone
furnace, after a plate in
Diderot's *Encyclopédie.* The
Encyclopédie, published
between 1751 and 1776,
devoted much space and many
engraved plates to a description of technical processes and
equipment used in the arts of
its day, and it was a widely
disseminated work of reference. The type of furnace
shown here was used in both
England and Germany in the
century following 1740. A
fairly complete example still
survives at Cutcliffe,
Yorkshire.

Opposite :
Pair of white opaque glass
vases enamelled with
chinoiseries with a Rococo
ornamental border, probably
painted in South Staffordshire, *c.* 1760. 'Rococo began
when the scrolls stopped being
symmetrical' is a useful key
to recognizing the style.
Chinoiseries, a favourite
Rococo theme, are fantasy
Chinese scenes invented by
European artists, and were
extremely popular from about
1725, when Johann Gregor
Höroldt introduced them at
Meissen, until about 1765.
The form of these vases is
based on Chinese porcelain,
and similar decoration can be
found on English porcelain of
the period and on enamels on
copper made in South
Staffordshire, where these
vases were probably painted.

G.1732.

porary, J. van Gool, to the effect of drawing with white chalk on coloured paper. In addition to Greenwood and Schumann, one of Greenwood's followers, David Wolff (1732–98), also left several signed specimens. Work of this kind was time-consuming, and could hardly have been a commercial proposition. It is interesting to note that all these people, including Anna Roemers Visscher and her sister, were talented amateurs, like Canon A. O. E. von dem Busch of Hildesheim, who in the eighteenth century did diamond engraving on glass and on white Meissen porcelain, filling the engraving with black pigment (*Schwarzlot*) to make it visible.

Mention must be made of glasses that were decorated calligraphically with broad flourishes by Anna Roemers Visscher and others, the decoration usually being executed on the type of goblet termed a *Römer*. These are very rare.

From Roman times onwards glass had been made in the Rhineland (the old Lotharingia), and at one time craftsmanship of a high order had been displayed by the glassworkers of Cologne. But after the ending of the Pax Romana only *Waldglas* was made, and much of the industry was transferred westwards to Lorraine. Rhineland glass always differed to some extent from that of the rest of Germany, and much of the surviving *Waldglas* originated there. The decoration of vessels like the *Igel* (the 'hedgehog' glass of the fifteenth and sixteenth centuries) in which the glass is drawn out into points, was the forerunner of the prunt, a form of decoration which especially occurs on the stem of seventeenth-century *Römers* (page 44). Those with a pattern of raised dots resembling the surface of a raspberry are called 'raspberry prunts', while some are impressed with the lion of St Mark, inspired by Venetian style. The stem of the early *Römer* was made by winding glass rod round a conical former which was removed before the bowl was welded to it. In the eighteenth century the conical former was made of glass, the rod being wound over it, which is a useful way of dating a glass approximately. The *Römer* (which is not the same type of glass as the late eighteenth- and nineteenth-century English *rummer*, despite the similarity in pronunciation of the two words) was the subject of a good deal of distinguished diamond-point and wheel-engraved decoration by Anna Roemers Visscher and others. There are a number of other glasses which were principally made in the Rhineland, notably the *Passglas*, a cylindrical glass with three equidistant rings of indented trailed glass around it, which was intended for communal drinking.

The styles of Venice had some influence on Rhineland glass, and the work of Venice and England also inspired a good deal of glass made at Liège by the Bonhomme family, who started in 1680, although glasshouses were working here at the beginning of the century. In Holland the first glasshouse to be influenced by Venice was established in Middleburg about 1530, and

Antwerp first made glass about 1550. The Dutch, however, were handicapped by the lack of wood fuel, and much of their attention was turned to decorating glass especially imported from England.

FRENCH GLASS

In the early days glassmaking in France was concentrated in Lorraine, Normandy, and Poitou, where *verre de fougère*, or fern glass, was made. Both Normandy and Lorraine were very early centres of the craft. The Italian glasshouse at Altare was originally established in the ninth century by craftsmen from Normandy who migrated southeastwards as a result of raids by the Northmen. They began to return in the fifteenth century, bringing with them some of the secrets of Venice, as well as those of Altare. Lorraine was among the earliest centres for the production of convex mirrors, a section cut from a blown sphere. These were being made as early as the thirteenth century, but probably the best-known example of a Lorraine mirror occurs in Jan van Eyck's *Marriage of Jan Arnolfini* in the National Gallery, London, which is dated 1434.

When Louis XIV built the Palace of Versailles the mirrors for the Galerie des Glaces were imported from Venice, but in 1693 Bernard Perrot, member of a family of Altarist glassmakers, devised a method of casting sheets of glass on a copper bed (plate glass) and France was the only source of fine quality mirror plate until the 1770's, when manufacture began in England also. Little good quality decorative and table glass was made until the end of the eighteenth century, and supplies were imported from Bohemia and England, but table glass of excellent quality was being made in France just before the Revolution began in 1789, and in the nineteenth century French glassworkers achieved an enviable reputation for decorative glass of all kinds, a departure which will be considered later. Especially noteworthy are the rare glass figures made 'at the lamp' in Nevers and Paris throughout the seventeenth century and into the nineteenth, finishing about 1845.

SPANISH GLASS

Glassmaking was an important craft in Spain in Roman times, and in later centuries Islamic and Venetian glass, and that of Bohemia, all influenced Spanish production. Islamic glass particularly influenced manufacture in Almeria and Granada, where glass was being made in the thirteenth century, but early specimens are very rare. Some of the forms, however, persisted till the seventeenth and even the eighteenth centuries. In Catalonia, especially at Barcelona, glass was being made in the fourteenth century, and the wares were favour-

ably compared with those of Venice. Enamelled glass influenced by Islamic designs was being produced by the fifteenth century, and by the eighteenth century crudely enamelled *Milchglas*, probably suggested by imports from Bohemia, was being made for export, especially to Mexico. A glasshouse at Cadalso (Toledo) was making glass in the seventeenth century in a variety of colours and forms, which, according to a contemporary writer, could compete with Venetian products, and the same factory imitated precious and semiprecious stones. The glass of San Martin de Valderglesias, which was made at a factory directed by a Belgian named Diodonet Lambot, also imitated Venetian styles, but the most important Spanish manufactory was La Granja de San Ildefonso, founded in 1728 under the patronage of Philip V and his consort, Isabel Farnese. This produced mirrors, chandeliers, and a variety of decorative objects for royal use, and, unlike other Spanish glass which was made in the tradition of the *vitrearius*, elaborately cut and engraved work was commonly done. Gilding was a speciality, and plate glass mirrors were being produced by 1770 or before.

Characteristically Spanish are such vessels as the *pórron*, a flat-based wine vessel with a long straight spout from which a stream of wine could be projected into the mouth; the *cántaro*, a closed water vessel with a ring handle on the top and two spouts, one for filling and the other for pouring; and the *almorrata*, or rose-water sprinkler, with a large neck and sprinkler spout rising from the shoulders, a type also made in Venice. These usually came from the province of Catalonia and are often decorated with *lattinicio* work.

Opposite, above:
English *Römer* decorated with the Four Seasons, from Greenwich, 1663. The Greenwich glasshouse employed Venetian glassmakers who worked in soda glass. John Evelyn refers to it as 'the Italian glasshouse . . . where glass was blown of finer metal than that of Murano'. The form of this *Römer* is unique. The engraving shows Netherlands influence but is probably English.

Opposite, below left:
Covered *Römer* with the monogram of the Swedish Queen Ulrika Eleonore, Kungsholm, Sweden, 1720. Like the *Pokal*, the *Römer* was originally covered, but the covers are now nearly always missing.

Opposite, below right:
Large covered *Römer* engraved with the Four Elements, South Germany, c. 1730. The Four Elements—earth, air, fire, and water—were a favourite symbolic theme in the 18th century.

Below:
Goblet with a view of the Phoenix glassworks, Bristol, early 19th century. Documentary specimens are always highly valued because of the light they throw on the provenance and date of other examples. Glasses of this kind include those that are signed or dated, those for which contemporary written records exist, or those, like this goblet, which can be definitely attributed because of the decoration.

Above :
Jug of pale green glass speckled with opal, Stourbridge, early 19th century. Jugs of this kind are traditionally associated with a glasshouse at Wrock-wardine in Shropshire, but they were also made at Stourbridge and attributed to Nailsea. They were a by-product of the bottle-making industry and some sealed bottles are decorated in this way.

Right :
Candle shade and gilt-bronze holder, France, early 19th century. The gilt-bronze holder is in the Empire style, *c.* 1810, and the shade is an early form of opaline painted in 'cold' colours with the typical Empire subject of Apollo and the chariot of the sun. This example is extremely rare.

Opposite :
Vase of blue glass decorated with a figure subject within an elaborate border in enamel colours and gilding, the ground dotted with *oeil de perdrix* (partridge-eye) ornament in the manner of Sèvres porcelain, Bristol, *c.* 1840. This vase was made at a time when the major English factories were imitating Sèvres porcelain, then much admired in England. Glass was unsuitable for the more intricate types of modelled ornament possible in porce-lain ; hence this vase is simple in form. But the Sèvres *gros bleu* ground of underglaze cobalt blue may be recognized in the colour of the glass, and the *oeil de perdrix* pattern was a familiar embellishment of this ground especially in the 18th century. The painting within the gilt border is in the style of the 1840's and the treatment suggests a painter trained in one of the porcelain factories, perhaps Coalport.

GLASS IN ENGLAND AND IRELAND

Whether glass was made in England in Roman times is still uncertain, although what appears to be the remains of a glass furnace has been excavated. It is probable that Roman Britain did not entirely depend on imports of glass from Gaul and the Rhineland, especially as wood fuel and suitable raw materials would not have been difficult to find. The first certain record we have, however, is the establishment of a glasshouse at Chiddingfold, in Sussex, where wood fuel was plentiful, and bracken and beechwood ash were a source of alkali. This was started in the fourteenth century with the aid of workmen from the Continent, and one, John le Alemayn (that is, 'the German'), probably came from the Rhineland. Lorraine glassmakers established themselves at Alfold, in Surrey, in the middle of the sixteenth century, and then went on to London. They made a soda glass with the aid of barilla imported from Spain which contained both lime and soda. A monopoly granted to them in 1567 speaks of the 'art, feate, or mystery of making glas such as is made in Fraunce, Lorayne, and Burgondy'. Eventually these Lorraine glassmakers settled in the area around Stourbridge, and a few went north as far as Newcastle-upon-Tyne.

In 1575 a glassmaker from Murano, Giacomo Verzelini, arrived in London from Antwerp, and was granted a monopoly by Queen Elizabeth I of making drinking glasses in the style of Murano for a term of 21 years. He first established himself at an existing glasshouse at Crutched Friars, in the City of London, and then transferred to Broad Street not far away. About eight glasses attributed to Verzelini have survived. The metal (a term commonly used to describe glass) is grey, with the usual imperfection of the period, and the diamond-point decoration may have been the work of Anthony de Lysle rather than of Verzelini himself. In 1592 Verzelini's glasshouse became the property of Sir Jerome Bowes, and it probably continued in operation into the early years of the seventeenth century.

In 1615 inroads into the forests in search of fuel reached a point where glassmakers were forbidden to use wood, and coal was employed instead. This led to the redesign of furnaces, and the open crucibles employed for wood-fired glass were replaced by covered, or 'crowned', crucibles which protect the contents from the sulphuric gases given off by coal. Vice-Admiral Sir Robert Mansell, a successful financier, bought up existing monopolies, and established a number of glasshouses in England which made glass with Spanish barilla, using coal as fuel and employing workmen from Altare. His enterprises do not seem to have survived the Civil War, and in 1663 George Villiers, Duke of Buckingham, petitioned Charles II for what was probably a renewal of

Mansell's monopoly. He opened a glasshouse at Vauxhall with the aid of a Frenchman, John le Cam, to make looking glasses and imitations of rock crystal.

The diarist, John Evelyn, was in Venice in June, 1645, where he records seeing glass of Murano and buying some to send to England by sea. He refers to white sand, flints from Pavia ground small, and the ashes of seaweed from Syria, which were the raw materials of the glass. In September 1676, he visited Buckingham's glasshouse at Lambeth where he saw 'looking-glasses far larger and better than any that came from Venice'. He refers, also, to 'huge vases of metal as clear, ponderous and thick as [rock] crystal'.

Survivals from this period are very few. Among the most notable are a small number of 'flutes', glasses of tall, narrow, conical form which may have originated in Holland. One is shown on page 52. They all belong to the years immediately following the Restoration of Charles II in 1662. The English market was partly being supplied by Venice, and an important correspondence survives between Alessio Morelli, a Venetian glassmaker, and John Greene, Warden of the Glass-Sellers' Company in 1677, who was importing glass from Venice. The letters include many drawings of the type of drinking glasses Greene was ordering. These were plain, simple and utilitarian, unlike the more spectacular types of Venetian glass with which Venice is usually associated. Those glasses of the type ordered by Greene which have survived are much heavier than the normal Venetian production,

probably because they had to withstand the hazards of sea transport. In 1671 Greene wrote to Morelli: 'We make now very good Drinking glasses in England' and he asked to be used 'very kindly' in the prices.

George Ravenscroft (1612–81) started an experimental glasshouse in the Savoy, London, in 1673, where he had the assistance of a worker from Altare. His intention was to make a crystal glass to rival that of the Venetians, and he was probably making a potash glass from flints calcined and ground to powder. Antonio Neri's handbook of glassmaking, the *Arte Vetraria*, had been translated into English in 1662, and Ravenscroft undoubtedly knew it. Flint was not a very fusible kind of silica, and at first Ravenscroft tried to overcome this by adding larger quantities of alkali, but this led to crisseling (page 21), a defect which reveals itself originally as a network of fine lines which will, unless the glass is kept in a dry atmosphere, eventually destroy it. To try to overcome this defect Ravenscroft substituted lead oxide for some of the potash, a process suggested by Neri. The addition of lead to pottery glazes was a very ancient practice, but hitherto, despite Neri's reference, it had rarely been employed to make glass, and then principally to produce imitation gemstones, although lead has been identified in some Roman glass. The effect of adding lead oxide was to increase the fusibility of the glass, but it was a long way from Venetian soda glass in its manipulative properties. Nor could it be blown with the same facility. It did, however, possess a brilliance even greater than that of rock crystal, although its particular suitability for facet cutting was not immediately realized. The patent granted to Ravenscroft in 1673 for a term of seven years refers to the glass's resemblance to rock crystal, and by arrangement with the Glass-Sellers' Company Ravenscroft set up a glasshouse at Henley-on-Thames. He adopted a seal mark of a raven's head, and by 1676 it was reported that crisseling had been overcome.

Ravenscroft died in 1681, and both the Henley and the Savoy glasshouses were taken over by Hawley Bishop, his assistant. The number of glasshouses making the new glass multiplied, the most important being in London, near the banks of the Thames, where supplies of raw material and coal could be brought easily and cheaply up the river. Both Venetian and German styles were current, but there are few specimens outside the cases of museums.

At this time Chinese porcelain was being imported into England in increasing quantities, and the potter John Dwight claimed to have found out the 'mistery' of making it. It is not, therefore, surprising to find a few specimens of glass opacified with tin oxide that are attributable to this period, especially as there were flourishing potteries making ware glazed with tin enamel at Southwark and Lambeth. In both of these places glasshouses flourished. A certain amount of coloured glass was also produced, but specimens are now very rare.

By 1700 Venetian influence had disappeared, and the craftsmen who came to England with William and Mary brought Dutch influence along with them. The accession of George I in

Above, left :
Pilgrim bottle of blue glass cased over opal, and decorated with an etched circular portrait within a laurel wreath, Stourbridge, *c.* 1855. The pilgrim bottle is found in pottery, porcelain and glass, and first occurs in ancient Roman pottery. Pilgrim bottles intended for use have two lugs on the shoulder but by the 19th century, whether made in glass or porcelain, they were generally ornamental survivals only and the handles for carrying them were omitted.

Above, right :
Vase cased with blue over crystal and enamelled with flowers, Stourbridge, *c.* 1860. Made to compete with porcelain, the underlying opal glass simulates the white porcelain surface and the blue a ground colour.

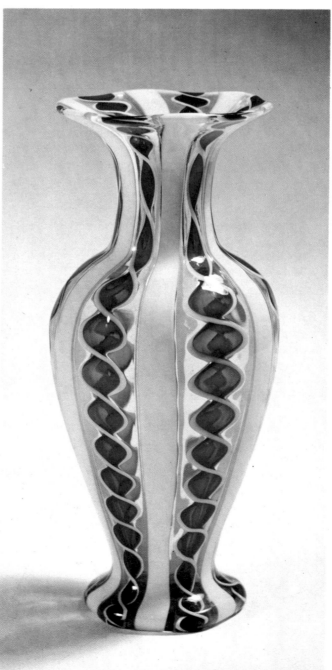

Below, left :
Cylindrical vase of orange-coloured glass with a strongly marked crackle effect and an iridized surface, Stourbridge, *c.* 1895. The iridized surface inspired by excavated glass became popular after Lobmeyr exhibited specimens in the Vienna Exposition of 1873. Experiment with surfaces, like the crackled effect shown here, was common from the 1880's onwards.

Below, right :
Vase decorated with six vertical canes interspersed with six white spiral canes, Stourbridge, *c.* 1840. Although the *latticinio* technique had died out by 1800, it was revived in Bohemia around 1840 and soon spread to other centres. The *Guide du Verrier* of Georges Bontemps, published in 1868, discusses the various techniques at length.

Opposite :
Vase coated with silver leaf and tinted yellow, rose and pale blue, with green trailing tendrils, Stourbridge, *c.* 1890. A colourful example of experimentation with forms and surface treatments which preoccupied glass-makers during the closing decades of the 19th century.

A notable series of enamelled glasses, painted by William Beilby, came from Newcastle, some of which are signed and dated. Coloured glass, and enamelled opaque white glass, came from Bristol and elsewhere. Most sought after is the enamelled white glass presumed to be from the hand of Michael Edkins (1734–1811), a glass and delft painter who was at work in Bristol from 1755 onwards, but similar work came from South Staffordshire, and the porcelain-decorating studio of James Giles in London also decorated glass with enamelling and gilding in characteristic style in the 1760's.

Although Irish glassmaking was on an appreciable scale in the seventeenth century, and Ravenscroft's lead glass had probably reached Dublin a little before 1700, the rise of Irish glassmaking at Waterford, Cork, and Belfast did not begin until 1780, when it became profitable to produce it there. The first important Waterford glasshouse was established in 1783. Three glasshouses were established in Cork, the first of which was also started in 1783. Cork glass is sometimes marked. The principal glasshouse in Belfast was established in 1776, and marked specimens are known.

AMERICAN GLASS

Glass was produced in America as early as 1607, when a glasshouse was established at Jamestown, Virginia, but little glass made before 1800 now survives, and production before this date was principally glass of domestic utility and window glass. Nevertheless, the products of three masters are much admired: those of Henry William Stiegel (1729–85) of Mannheim, Pennsylvania, who flourished between 1763 and 1774, some of whose glass was decorated with enamelling and engraving; those of Caspar Wistar (1739–52) of Salem County, New York, whose glasshouse closed about 1780, which cannot be identified with certainty; and those of John Frederick Amelung, whose glasshouse was at New Bremen, Maryland, from 1785 to 1795. All were men of German origin, who worked largely in a German tradition. American glass of the nineteenth century is discussed in the final chapter of this book.

This is a brief, and necessarily lacunary, review of the history of glass, but from it emerge a few generalizations of importance. The first is the influence of the type of glass employed— soda glass, potash glass, or lead glass—on the nature of the production. Each lends itself to a particular kind of work which cannot so effectively be produced in glass of any other kind, although potash glass and lead glass are perhaps interchangeable for certain purposes.

Another important point is that even today the skill of the craftsman is just as essential to work of high quality as it always has been, and

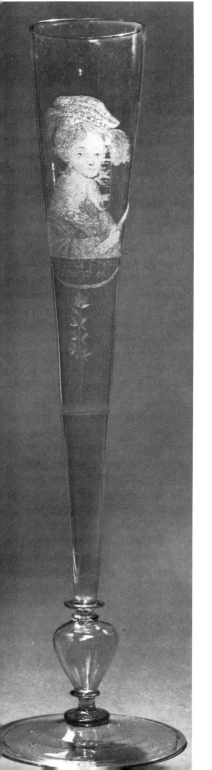

1714 brought a fresh influx of northern craftsmen, and a preference for German styles, and the industry in England appeared to be set on a flourishing course when disaster struck, in the form of taxation imposed by the Glass Excise Act of 1745. This tax was on the weight of the *materials* used in the making of lead glass, and it had the effect of forcing manufacturers to make vessels which were thin, light in weight, and with little or no decoration. The best facet cutting needed to be done on thick-walled, and therefore heavy vessels, which allowed plenty of metal to cut away, and these paid a correspondingly heavier duty. Since the Act did not include Ireland, English glassmakers began to open manufactories there to supply the Irish market, and the doubling of the duty in 1780 coincided with the Irish Trade Treaty which allowed glass to be exported to England free of duty. This gave a considerable inducement to the Irish glasshouses to manufacture for export, and craftsmen from Stourbridge and Bristol left to work in Ireland. Inducements also persuaded English glassmakers to emigrate to France before the Revolution to help promote the table-glass industry there. This damaging tax was eventually removed in 1845, and the almost instantaneous growth of the English glass industry which followed was clear proof of the stunting effect it had had for so long.

Because of the tax the cut glass made in England in the last quarter of the eighteenth century favoured slender shapes and shallow cutting, and heavy pieces, deeply cut, are usually Irish. Thick, heavy bases to bowls on pedestals are also evidence of an Irish origin.

Among the most highly valued English glasses are those engraved with emblems and portraits relating to King William III—the so-called Williamite glasses, and those made for the Jacobite supporters of the Old and Young Pretenders. Some of the latter were probably engraved in Holland on glass from Newcastle.

there have been few technical advances on the old methods of forming and decorating glass. Those which have occurred during the last 150 years have largely been chemical—the introduction of new fluxes for particular purposes, and new colours. Automatic manufacturing processes have largely been limited to the production of utilitarian glass, especially pottery.

Although it was not until the invention of glass blowing that it became possible to exploit the peculiar properties of glass to the full, it has nearly always been valued for its properties of light refraction, more so perhaps than for its plastic qualities, and this has led to its employment as an imitation of semiprecious hardstones. Its resemblance when uncoloured to rock crystal is particularly important, and the simulation of this stone was often the intention of the earlier glassmakers. It led to the decoration of glass by the same methods as those employed by hardstone carvers, the Roman *diatretarii*. In work of this kind the carving and engraving is necessarily the most important aspect, even though the foundation on which it is executed was the work of the glass blower, the *vitrearius*. There have been some, John Ruskin especially, who have contended that the art of the *vitrearius* was the only true one, and this pronouncement led to the decline of the art of cutting glass in the second half of the nineteenth century. But the stricture is unjustified. The two techniques represent entirely different aspects of the art. In carving no greater virtue resides in the use of a natural stone than in the employment of a man-made substance.

The technique of enamelling on glass is akin to that of enamelling on pottery and porcelain glazes, or on copper, and the only difference is in the material employed. In the case of the former, there is almost no difference between the techniques because pottery and porcelain glazes are both forms of glass.

It is difficult, for the most part, to classify many specimens of glass as belonging definitely to the period of the Baroque, Rococo, or Classical styles by their form alone, as may be done with much pottery and porcelain, although decoration may have the elements of one or other of these styles. Consequently, this kind of stylistic evidence is not always available for dating. The more highly decorated the glass the easier it is to date. The most difficult to date are plain glasses of simple form. Certain early glasses have been reproduced in the past century or so, but few of them will deceive anyone well acquainted with genuine specimens, and some reproductions, such as those of certain Roman glass, were not intended to deceive in the first place, and are not difficult to detect. They are, however, sometimes sold in Italy to unsuspecting tourists under the guise of ancient glass.

Glass is essentially a Western craft, apart from the work of Near Eastern glassmakers of the early and medieval period. The Chinese nearly always treated glass as though it were a substance akin to jade or porcelain, and either carved or enamelled it by methods appropriate to those crafts. In later times, from the beginning of the seventeenth century onwards, glass influenced by Venetian work was made in Persia, apparently with the aid of Venetian glassworkers, because their presence in that country is recorded.

Little nineteenth-century factory-made glass can be regarded as artistically important, but it has become of great and increasing interest to collectors, principally because specimens of earlier work have become increasingly difficult to obtain. Towards the end of the century, more or less parallel with such movements as Art Nouveau, which saw a revival of the art of glass and Impressionism in the field of painting, we have the work of men like Emile Gallé which is now much admired. This is discussed later.

Wine and Drinking Glasses

Goblet of dark purple glass with trailed ornament, the circlet, foot and stem of silver, Venice, mid-16th century. The silver mounts are of a later date, no doubt to repair damage to the stem and foot. This goblet is traditionally associated with Bishop Ridley of Oxford (d. 1555).

The custom of using glasses for serving wine is an ancient one. Pliny records that, in his day, vessels of gold and silver were being abandoned in favour of those made of glass, and some of the prices he records for the rarer drinking glasses compare very closely with those realized for similar vessels in the precious metals. Very few have survived, and most of these are of tumbler shape. The existence of goblets on a stem and foot can perhaps be inferred from Pliny's descriptions, but difficulties of translation make this uncertain. The Lycurgus Cup in the British Museum has the remains of a low, splayed foot, but no stem. A number of conical, facet-cut beakers have survived which stand on a slightly splayed foot of narrow diameter.

The era known as the Dark Ages, after the fall of Rome, seems to have been a period of heavy drinking, because most survivals are drinking glasses of one kind or another. The claw beaker of the sixth century, a conical beaker of about the same date which is a survival of a Roman type, and the drinking horn are examples of Frankish glass drinking vessels, and it is noteworthy that, with the doubtful exception of the first, none of these could have been put down unemptied.

The Hedwig glasses (page 29) and enamelled beakers such as the 'Luck of Edenhall' are examples of Islamic drinking glasses, but the first European glasses to survive that have a stem and foot are the enamelled goblets of fifteenth-century Venice. The fourteenth-century Bolognese fresco already mentioned, however, shows a figure holding a clear glass of this kind with a shallow, wide bowl somewhat like that of a modern champagne glass. A sixteenth-century 'Last Supper' by Bonifacio Veronese at Bassano not only shows glasses of this type on the table, but also wine decanters with a pedestal foot and a handle from which the glasses were filled.

Venetian glasses in the sixteenth and seventeenth centuries became very elaborate, with a convoluted stem which was often extremely complex, and a foot folded over at the edge (folded foot) for greater strength. The decoration of these glasses with diamond-point engraving has already been discussed. By far the greater part of Venetian production must have been devoted to plain glasses with a conical, bucket-shaped bowl, a short, knopped stem, and a spreading foot. This was the type being principally imported by John Greene of London in the 1670's, which he asked to be made thick and heavy to withstand the hazards of transport by sea, and the type, termed Anglo-Venetian, was also made in England. Common glasses of this kind were not cared for as tenderly as those that were more elaborately decorated, and few have survived.

The Germans obviously inherited the love of Frankish glassmakers for wine and ale. Many of their drinking glasses are so large that they are obviously aleglasses. One could hardly imagine a glass of the capacity of the *Reichsadlerhumpen* being used for any other purpose. German and Netherlandish vessels of this kind took many forms. For wine drinking, the Netherlands glasshouses made goblets *façon de Venise* (a goblet is a glass holding more than four ounces of liquid), but the German glasshouses usually preferred the *Römer* (or *Roemer*; both spellings are correct). Römer glasses made in the Netherlands usually have a conical bowl terminating in a cylinder not unlike the German version but without the conical, spirally wound foot. Either version is usually decorated with prunts, in the Netherlands version on the lower, cylindrical part. Enamelling, and calligraphic and wheel engraving decorated seventeenth-century German drinking glasses, and particularly esteemed are tumblers or beakers painted by the *Hausmaler*. Towards the end of the seventeenth century a much more sophisticated type of engraved decoration (*Hochschnitt* and *Tiefschnitt*) was applied to the kind of covered drinking-glass termed a *Pokal*. This, a purely German shape, was derived from standing silver cups by such Renaissance silversmiths as Wenzel Jamnitzer, a sixteenth-century Viennese who worked at Nürnberg. A representative selection of this very important category is illustrated on pages 44 and 45, and all are noted for the quality of the engraving, which is in the contemporary Baroque style. Covered *Römer* and tumblers similarly decorated also exist, but are rare. The principal sources of engraving of this kind are Bohemia and Silesia, Potsdam, and Hesse.

Belonging to the first half of the eighteenth century are the beakers, and an occasional

Pokal, of the type known as *Zwischengoldgläser* (literally, gold between glasses) with two glasses fitting precisely together, the exterior of the inner glass being covered with gold or silver leaf (the latter termed *Zwischensilbergläser*) engraved with a design, sometimes in conjunction with painting in colour, which is protected by the outer glass. It is possible that at least some of these glasses, especially those decorated with Christian subjects, were made in an unidentified Bohemian monastery. Later work by the Austrian, Johann Josef Mildner (1763–1808), made use of a related technique by which he inserted medallions into a space cut to receive them, and backed them with either gold leaf or red lacquer (page 20).

Dutch glassmakers in the eighteenth century produced some excellent stipple and linear diamond engraving on wineglasses by David Wolff and others, and English glasses from Newcastle were often employed in Holland for this purpose. These, of course, are extremely scarce, and, like the German engraved glasses, only rarely come onto the market.

Good quality crystal tableware, including wineglasses, was being produced in France towards the end of the eighteenth century, largely inspired by Bohemian and English production, which supplied the bulk of French requirements of this kind.

Before leaving the subject of Continental drinking glasses, reference should be made to the opaque white glass mugs, straight-sided with handles and decorated with enamelling in the manner of porcelain, which were made at Basdorf, near Potsdam, or in Bohemia. The Basdorf glasshouse was founded because the proprietors could not obtain permission to start a porcelain factory, and its products were designed to compete with porcelain rather than glass. It also made most of the pieces normally included in a tea service, including cups and saucers, tea jars, bowls, and so on, but glass was otherwise hardly ever employed for this purpose because glass teapots could not withstand boiling water without cracking. The one or two cut-glass English specimens which survive from the eighteenth century must have been intended as punchpots for this reason, as were many of the large contemporary pots of porcelain and earthenware. The characteristic European teapot was, of course, an adaptation of the Chinese winepot to a new purpose in the seventeenth century.

The earliest English wineglasses to survive are the diamond-engraved glasses of Verzelini made towards the end of the sixteenth century, of which about eight are known. A few *façon de Venise* glasses survive from the seventeenth century, made either in the Netherlands or in England of soda glass, most of them similar in style to those being imported by John Greene from Venice.

Towards the end of the seventeenth century, when Ravenscroft's lead glass had come into

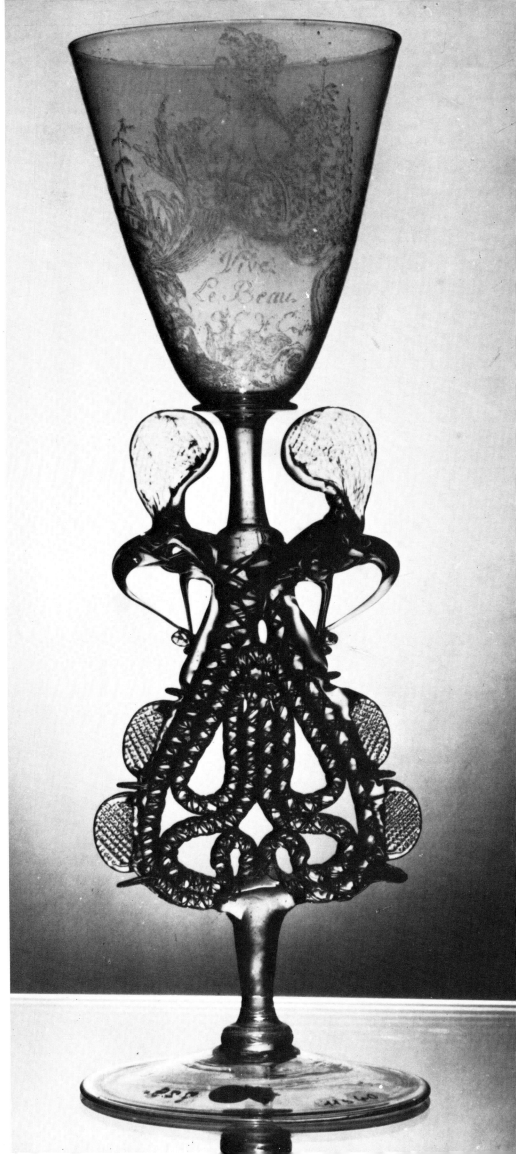

Above:
Zwischengoldglas beaker, Bohemia, *c.* 1735. This is a revival of an ancient technique of sandwiching gold leaf between two sheets of glass, which may have been Jewish in origin, and was continued by Jewish glass-makers in Byzantium. The British Museum has a bowl dating from the 2nd or 3rd century AD. Surviving 18th-century work is more or less limited to beakers and covered *Pokals,* the gold work usually in conjunction with 'cold' colours and sometimes with coloured glass. Not infrequently silver replaces gold leaf, when the term *Zwischen-silberglas* is used. A similar technique was employed by Johann Josef Mildner towards the end of the 18th century for glass with medallions inset.

Below:
Ochsenkopf (ox-head) beaker, German enamelled glass dated 1644. The Ochsenkopf is a mountain in the Fichtelgebirge of Bavaria, and its pine-clad slopes are depicted on the glass. Near the base are two of the four rivers which rise there, the others being shown on the reverse side. They are the Saal, Main, Naab and Eger.

Opposite:
Römer of green glass painted with an engagement between English and Dutch men-of-war, Netherlands, inscribed *Michael de Ruyter* and dated 1667. This very rare glass commemorates the exploit of Michael Adrianszoon de Ruyter, the Dutch admiral who sailed up the Medway in 1667 and burned some ships berthed at Rochester. He followed this by sailing up the Thames as far as Gravesend, whence the thunder of his guns could be clearly heard in the city of London, and then he turned for home, attacking Harwich on his way.

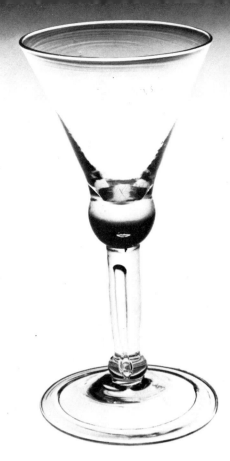

general use, small aleglasses appear, of conical form on a short stem and a folded foot in the Venetian manner. The bottom two thirds of the glass was often decorated with spiral ribbing, a feature contemporaries termed 'wrythen'. Later aleglasses are sometimes a little difficult to separate from wineglasses, but when they are engraved with the hopvine, its flowers, and the barley plant, their purpose is undoubted. Eighteenth-century aleglasses are usually small because the ale was much stronger than today's watery brews, and it was drunk in quantities very little greater than the customary amount of wine. For table use ale was drawn from the cask into decanters similarly engraved.

The subject of English drinking glasses is vast, and in this chapter it is only possible to review the subject briefly. The reader wishing to make a detailed study is commended to L. M. Bickerton's *Eighteenth Century Drinking Glasses*, published in 1971, which covers the subject with 854 black and white illustrations. Here, it is only possible to mention a few of the principal types and features.

By 1700 the principal wineglass stem formation was a type known as the 'baluster', the first examples of which occur about 1685. These, despite the name, are variable in form, and may have additional knops and rings. The baluster, also, is often inverted. A slender elongated type of baluster, especially found on glasses from Newcastle, is termed 'balustroid', and these are found between 1725 and 1755. The 'Silesian' stem, current from 1715 to 1765 but rarely seen after about 1745, is sometimes called a moulded pedestal stem. Most instances of the later use of this stem are sweetmeat glasses. The plain, straight stem became fashionable about 1740, and air-twist stems were introduced about the same time, to be followed about 1750 by stems with a twist incised on the exterior. Opaque twist stems first occur about the same time, and mixed and colour twist stems about five years afterwards. Stems of this kind are always straight with, at most, a simple knop at top or bottom, or in the middle. Air twists were produced by making a number of indentations in the bottom of a cylindrical piece of glass, followed by covering them with a layer of molten glass. The cylinder was then drawn out and twisted to the required length. Opaque white and colour twists were formed by arranging rods of the required colour in a mould and casing them with clear glass, followed by drawing out and twisting. Hat-banded twists are similarly formed. The technique has much in common with the making of *latticinio* and *millefiori* glass discussed elsewhere.

Copies of opaque white and colour twists are common today. Apart from other characteristics of eighteenth-century glass which they fail to reproduce, it is noteworthy that the twists are deeply buried in the stem, whereas genuine twists appear closely to approach its surface, some so closely as to seem to touch it.

Faceted stems were introduced in 1760 as a result of the growing popularity of cut glass. Not all faceted stems were cut at the time of manufacture, however. Composite stems usually belong to the period of the 1750's, and are built-up from several different types of stem, which are usually knopped, based on air twists or opaque twists. The type is quite rare.

Opposite, above left :
Pokal engraved with a view of Breslau, Silesian, *c.* 1730. This fine example of topographical engraving is carried on the Silesian stem which, with modifications, was employed for English glasses after George I acceded to the throne in 1714. In England this form of stem was more often used for sweetmeat glasses and is relatively unusual as a wineglass stem.

Opposite, above right :
Goblet with thistle-shaped bowl, air bubbles in the knop and stem and a folded foot, English, *c.* 1715. The enclosed 'tear' or air bubble was widely used as a form of decoration. The workman dented the glass at this point and covered the depression with a layer of glass. The subsequent form was modified by manipulation, as, for example, when the stem was drawn out from the base of the bowl.

Opposite, below :
Ale glass with wrythen moulding (i.e., fine spiral reeding) and a folded foot, English, late 17th century. The wrythen ornament of this glass first occurs as far back as the 5th century, and forms a simple decoration for an otherwise plain glass. examples are rare and date from the years on either side of 1700.

Right :
Ale flute with air-twist stem, English, *c.* 1770. The air twist is largely an English form of decoration, which started about 1740. Air twists are usually to be found in the drawn shank type of glass (see page 10).

Far right :
Wineglass with white and green twist stem and knops at the top and in the centre, English, *c.* 1780. A favourite type of glass with collectors, with the result that forgeries are not uncommon.

The plain stem was drawn out from the bottom of the bowl and the foot added. Air twists were made in the same way. Other glasses, such as the baluster stems, and the Silesian stems, were made in three parts—bowl, stem, and foot—welded together. Careful inspection will usually reveal welded joints, but these may also occur in the case of repaired glasses.

There were at least 20 different types of bowl in reasonably common use. They all have names descriptive of the shape—bell-shaped, waisted, bucket-shaped, conical, thistle-shaped, funnel, trumpet, ogee, to name but a few. The types of stem referred to are found with a variety of bowls, except for the straight stem. This nearly always had a trumpet-shaped or round funnel bowl from the base of which the stem was drawn out. Feet, also, take a number of forms. The Venetian folded foot occurred often until about 1745, after which it disappeared for several years, and returned again for a period of very limited use towards the end of the century. The edge of the foot was turned *under* to form a double thickness which increased the strength at this point. Continental glasses were frequently thus turned *over*, and the amount turned was less in width than with English glasses. English glasses sometimes had a domed foot folded at the edge, which is known as a domed and folded foot.

The formation of a typical wineglass begins with a bulb of glass with a solid blob at one end drawn out to form the stem, to which the foot is attached. The tool which grips the foot is termed the *gadget*, and, holding the glass in this way, the gaffer would trim the edge of the bowl with shears, and shape it with a pair of tongs called a *pucelas*. This sequence of operations may vary with the type of glass being made, and

with the methods of the team making it. Eighteenth-century glasses may be examined by running the finger round the rim where the point where the shears closed to make their last cut will usually be apparent as a slight irregularity; there may be tong marks on the bowl, and the gadget leaves pressure marks on the foot.

A roughened patch in the centre of the foot marks the point where the glass was broken off from the pontil rod. This is present on most eighteenth-century glasses, especially those made during the early years. The underside of the eighteenth-century foot is concave in section to a greater or lesser extent, so the pontil mark rarely interfered with the firm standing of the glass, but an obtrusive pontil mark necessitated grinding, and eventually it became customary to remove it altogether. A foot more or less flat underneath, to be found on many Victorian glasses, then became possible.

Most English wineglasses are plain, and many were probably intended for tavern use, but diamond engraving, wheel engraving, cutting, enamelling, and gilding are all to be found decorating eighteenth-century specimens, and etched ornament was introduced in the nineteenth century. Coloured glasses, of which the commonest colours are green and blue, are to be found from the middle of the eighteenth century onwards, some a combination of clear and coloured glass. These probably came mostly from Bristol in the eighteenth century and from Stourbridge in the nineteenth.

Many English engraved glasses are commemorative in one way or another, the most important group being the Jacobite glasses decorated with portraits of Prince Charles Edward, the Jacobite rose, the Scottish thistle,

Above :
Bohemian tumbler, wineglass and candlestick decorated *en suite, c.* 1840. Part of a table service of ruby-cased crystal glass decorated with wheel engraving—a type popular in England at mid century.

Below, left :
Bohemian goblet cased with ruby glass and engraved with a fox and cubs, the opposite side with small diminishing lenses through which the decoration may be viewed in miniature. This is a rare and exceptionally well decorated example of ruby-cased glass, which was still being made by the end of the 19th century, although by then quality had deteriorated. Much of it was engraved with views of spas and sold as a kind of souvenir.

Below, right :
Another view of the same glass through the diminishing lenses, which concentrate the light and give a sharp image of the decoration. The goblet is characteristic of the Bohemian glass exported to England between 1830 and 1850, although of considerably better quality than most. Engravers set up shop in the Bohemian spas where they engraved glasses and sold them to visitors. In 1842 Friedrich Egermann employed 200 workmen who, between them, engraved 2,500 tons of glass every year.

Opposite :
Bell-shaped goblet cased with ruby glass in the Bohemian style with hollow baluster stem. The glass was designed and engraved by W. Muckley, made by John Richardson of Wordsley and exhibited in the Great Exhibition of 1851. Bohemian glass of this type enjoyed considerable success at the Exhibition, and a number of journals, including *The Times,* castigated English glassmakers for the poor quality of their imitations of Bohemian work, advising manufacturers to buy some models for their workmen to copy. These criticisms, however, could hardly have been directed towards this goblet, which is exceptional in quality.

and other symbolic emblems. The very rare 'Amen' glasses are engraved with a verse or two of the Jacobite version of 'God save the King', followed by 'Amen'. Some Jacobite glasses are inscribed '*Audentior Ibo*', which, although often said to mean 'I will go more boldly next time', is, as it stands, meaningless. In an earlier work I suggested it might be an engraver's error for *Audentior Bibo* (I drink boldly), but Mr Joseph Scholles has since pointed out to me the confusion likely to arise in the eighteenth century between the script *b* and *t*, and he suggests instead it might be an engraver's erroneous reading of *Audentior ito*, which could in fact be translated 'Go more boldly (next time)'. This reading receives additional confirmation from the fact that it was the Sibyl's advice to Aeneas, and we may assume, therefore, that the wanderings and misfortunes of Prince Charles were being compared with those of Aeneas. This was an allusion to Virgil's *Aeneid* which would not have escaped the classically educated man of the eighteenth century.

'Williamite' glasses commemorate William III, prince of the house of Orange, and the Battle of the Boyne. Some are engraved with an orange tree, some with a portrait of William III. The Orange in question, incidentally, was the small southern French principality inherited in 1531 by the House of Nassau, to which William belonged. All these glasses are rare.

Glasses bearing a portrait of Frederick the Great can be dated fairly precisely to 1757, during the Seven Years War, when the Worcester factory made dated porcelain mugs that were similarly decorated. Frederick was so popular in England at the time that Horace Walpole remarked that he thought the common people believed him to be the King of England as well. Glasses exist commemorating naval battles and commanders, and such events as elections, and these can often be dated fairly precisely.

Cordial glasses are a well-defined category with bowls of the shapes customary for wineglasses, but much smaller, holding little more than an ounce of liquid. Cordials were the eighteenth-century equivalent of the twentieth-century cocktail, made by fermenting fruit juices; one of them, ratafia, made from almond kernels, was served in a special glass, with an elongated, waisted bowl, hardly larger at the top than the thickness of the stem. Apart from the size of the bowls, Cordial glasses resemble contemporary wineglasses probably because they were made *en suite*. They were first made in the seventeenth century, and continued to be popular throughout the eighteenth. They are therefore found in many styles. Perhaps the most usual, however, are those with opaque twist stems.

Rummers (the word itself derives from the German *Römer*, rather than from the liquor which was put in them) were popular from the

Left, above:
Wheel-engraved wineglass with air-twist stem, *c.* 1750. A type sometimes termed an '*Amen glass*'. The word, originally from Hebrew, means 'So be it', so it was the obvious answer to a toast given to 'The king across the water'. The much rarer and more elaborate glasses are engraved in diamond point with the crown and verses of the Jacobite anthem.

Left, below:
Cordial glass with an air-twist stem, English, *c.* 1760. The first mention of the term *cordial* seems to have been in 1663, and the last was probably a notice dated 1833 posted in a Cork glasshouse. The general design of cordial glasses was always the same: a small bowl on a tall stem, usually with a high foot.

Opposite, above left:
Wineglass engraved with a portrait of Prince Charles Edward Stuart, and the words *Audentior Ibo*, English, *c.* 1750. This type of glass, again, is a Jacobite relic, and the significance of the Latin text is discussed on this page.

Opposite, above centre:
Wineglass with an air-twist stem engraved with the Jacobite rose, English, *c.* 1750.

Opposite, above right:
Rummer decorated with engraving of Sunderland Bridge, English, *c.* 1796. A documentary glass, which can be dated with certainty around the time that Sunderland Bridge was opened in 1796. The bridge frequently appears on pottery of this period also.

Opposite, below:
Large wheel-engraved glass bearing the name of Robert Hancock, 1769. Glasses made for named individuals, and dated, are not at all uncommon in pottery and porcelain, but they are rarer in glass. It is a permissible speculation that this one may have been made for Robert Hancock, the engraver who was responsible for much Worcester transfer-printed porcelain of the period.

end of the eighteenth century till the middle of the nineteenth century. Ravenscroft's *Römers* were copied from those of seventeenth-century Germany, with spreading foot and prunts adorning the hollow stem. The rummer of the end of the eighteenth century, however, had become a glass with an unusually capacious bowl, a short stem of variable shape, and either a circular foot, or a heavy square foot, often with 'lemon squeezer' moulding inside it, quite unrelated to the earlier type. Many rummers are plain, but some are decorated with wheel engraving. One depicting Sunderland Bridge, which was opened in 1796 and served frequently as a subject of pottery decoration, can be dated fairly precisely (above). Engraved decoration considerably increases the value of a rummer.

Enamelled wineglasses are scarce, and those most sought are the work of William (1740–1819) and Mary (1749–97) Beilby of Newcastle. Their father was a silversmith who established himself in Durham, and William learned the art of enamelling in Birmingham. Much of William's early work took the form of coats of arms, sometimes for commemorative purposes, but his later work, in which Mary assisted, included landscapes, exotic birds, and pastoral subjects, either in white monochrome or colour. The signature, however, is always 'Beilby', and it is impossible to differentiate between the work of brother and sister. Their work was executed between 1762 and 1778, and includes both wineglasses and decanters.

Firing glasses are rarely decorated. They are so called because they were used for the drinking of toasts, and after they had been drained

Left :
Wineglass with bucket-shaped bowl and air-twist stem, enamelled by Beilby with the arms of Buckmaster of Lincoln, *c.* 1765. William and Mary Beilby of Newcastle-on-Tyne are the best-known 18th-century enamellers on glass. William learned the art of enamelling in Birmingham with a maker of small boxes of copper decorated with painted enamels, and his brother Ralph was a wood engraver who specialized in heraldic subjects. No doubt he influenced his brother and sister to specialize in this also. As the signature on these glasses is simply *Beilby,* it is impossible to separate the work of brother and sister, but Mary was much younger than William (she was 16 in 1765) so the armorial glasses are probably almost entirely his. The painting of rustic scenes and landscapes, done about 1774, are no doubt partly the work of Mary. The Beilbys employed a characteristic white enamel which is usually bluish in shade, but sometimes slightly pink in tone. They worked on locally made glasses of a type that was also exported to Holland for the addition of engraved decoration.

Opposite :
Opaque white glass beaker enamelled with figures after D'Hancarville, Bristol glass, *c.* 1770. Pierre Germain Hugues, Baron Han, who called himself D'Hancarville, acquired a dubious reputation as a wanderer in Italy in the 1760's. He ingratiated himself with Sir William Hamilton, the British envoy at Naples (and husband of Emma), and edited an illustrated work on Hamilton's collection of Etruscan, Greek and Roman antiquities which influenced several designers and manufacturers, such as Josiah Wedgwood, who used it for his pottery. Many of the motifs of the Neoclassical style employed between 1770 and 1790 were based on this work but D'Hancarville's knowledge was deficient and some of his statements highly inaccurate.

they were returned to the table with a loud rapping which suggested a ragged volley of musketry. Conical ice-cream glasses with a heavy base, common in the 1930's, are sometimes sold to unsuspecting novices as firing glasses. Toastmasters' glasses have thickened walls and a much thicker bottom to the bowl than is customary. They held a smaller quantity of liquor than ordinary glasses of the same size because the toastmaster had to drain every toast, and his function made it essential for him to stay on his feet till the end.

Wineglasses attributable to the Irish glasshouses are uncommon and tumblers are more frequent, which is perhaps indicative of the Irish taste for whiskey rather than wine. They are usually decorated with engraving or cutting, and heavily cut specimens belong principally to the period between 1810 and 1830 when the heavy cutting of thick glass was fashionable. Certainly identifiable plain wineglasses from Ireland cannot be said to exist, although seemingly they are represented in some of the surviving pattern books. Cordial glasses (known as dram glasses) were a popular Irish product.

During the nineteenth century wineglasses were increasingly made in large sets comprising at least a dozen of everything—port and sherry glasses, burgundy and claret glasses, champagne glasses and those for liqueurs, and the accompanying decanters. Much glass of this kind was cut or engraved at first, but elaborate cutting became unfashionable after Ruskin had pronounced against it. Towards the turn of the century glasses became light and slender, and Art Nouveau glasses were often made in forms

reminiscent of flowers. Stourbridge glassmakers made a tremendous quantity of cranberry (ruby-coloured) wineglasses in the second half of the century with plain bowls, stems, and feet. These are not uncommon today, and can be found singly or in half dozens. Table glass of the nineteenth century is usually bought for use rather than as collectors' pieces.

Among the ancillary glassware which contributed to the pleasures of drinking may be included the punch bowl, which was customarily made of silver or porcelain and only occasionally of glass, and the toddy lifter, always of glass, which was employed to serve (or 'lift') punch from the bowl into the glass. Toddy lifters are about six inches in length, shaped like a miniature decanter with an opening from top to bottom. The bottom part of the toddy lifter was immersed in the liquid and allowed to fill. The thumb was placed over the orifice at the top, which prevented the liquid from escaping. It was then transferred to a point over the glass and the thumb removed, allowing the contents to flow into the bowl. This simple device replaced the toddy ladle of silver of which some rare early specimens made in glass survive.

Monteiths—glass coolers with a scalloped rim from which the bowls were suspended by the foot in icewater—are very rarely of glass, but a type of small individual glass cooler, cylindrical with a lip on either side for two glasses, is not uncommon. These are often of blue glass, probably from Bristol, sometimes with a simple gilded key-fret ornament. They were popular towards the end of the eighteenth century. Posset and caudle pots are covered

Above, left:
Small glass cooler, for two glasses, bearing the arms of the Earl of Verulam, by Isaac Jacob, Bristol, early 19th century.

Above, right:
Wine cooler of silver pattern with shell handles, mirrored silver inside, accompanied by a loose crystal glass lining, Stourbridge, mid-19th century.

Opposite, above:
Monteith (a wineglass cooler) of Irish glass, late 18th century. The stem of the wineglass rested in the notch between the projections on the rim and was held in place by its foot. The bowl was immersed in ice water. Ice was procurable throughout the year by means of the age-old device of the ice pit, in which slabs of ice cut from the rivers and ponds during the winter were stored.

Opposite, below left:
Sweetmeat glass decorated with shallow cutting on a Silesian stem, English, *c.* 1735. 'Scollop'd Desart Glasses in the newest fashion' were advertised in 1737, and the earliest were probably made around 1714. Nevertheless, specimens which can be definitely regarded as earlier than 1740 are very uncommon.

vessels which have two handles and a pouring
spout. They were also made in tin-enamelled
pottery from Lambeth or Bristol, and date from
a period towards the end of the seventeenth
century until the middle of the eighteenth.
Posset and caudle were somewhat similar drinks
prepared from curdled milk and ale or wine
with the addition of various spices. Ravenscroft
specimens are much esteemed. These drinks
were usually consumed by sucking them
through the spout.

Sweetmeat glasses, part of the dessert service,
although they were employed for serving can-
died fruits, trifles, and similar sweets, so much
resemble contemporary wineglasses as to de-
serve consideration here. The decoration is
often more elaborate and of better quality than
in wineglasses of equivalent date, and the bowls
are considerably larger and shallower. Some
have been erroneously described as champagne
glasses. *Epergnes* or centrepieces, more familiar
in silver, had a number of arms projecting from
a central stem on which sweetmeat baskets
were hung from the handle provided.

Syllabub was a drink prepared from frothing
cream to which was added wine or sherry. At
first syllabubs were probably served in a
posset pot, but after the middle of the eighteenth
century a type of glass with a capacious bowl
and a short stem, sometimes with handles on
either side, was used instead. These are virtually
indistinguishable from the jelly glass, and the
two were probably interchangeable. Glasses in
which the bowl broadens out about halfway up
into a cup shape are, however, syllabub
glasses without any question.

Bottles and Flasks

The bottle as a container for liquids is the oldest of all glass vessels. The earliest known examples are small bottles from Egypt, probably perfume containers dating from the fifteenth century BC. These were made by attaching a sand core to a metal rod, followed either by dipping the core into molten glass, or by winding softened glass rod round it. By reheating, and rolling it on a flat surface, the surface was then smoothed and consolidated.

The invention in Syria of blowing into two- or three-piece moulds greatly facilitated the manufacture of bottles to contain wines, oil, perfumes, and so on. This was well established by the first century AD. Bottles of square section were made for easy and safe transport, and those of circular section were jacketed with woven straw for the same reason. Some were moulded with designs such as grapes, shells, and human heads, a fashion which was revived in the nineteenth century. Some bottles bear the name of the maker and this is the earliest known instance of the use of a trademark. In the Middle Ages wherever glassmakers set up their furnaces they made bottles of one kind or another, and these, along with drinking glasses, formed the principal product. Decorative but sometimes impractical bottles and flasks came from Venice.

The popularity of the glass bottle was largely due to the difficulty of making an earthenware bottle that was sufficiently glazed inside to prevent it from absorbing liquid, and even from leaking. These disadvantages were overcome in sixteenth-century Germany by the introduction of impervious stoneware bottles for wine and ale, and these were extremely popular throughout Western Europe, some of them even finding their way to Japan, where they were much appreciated by the *daimyos*. Rhineland stoneware bottles bore an oval moulded medallion with a variety of devices adapted to the requirements of the buyer, and it is probable that this inspired the addition of medallions, usually termed *seals*, to glass bottles.

England, however, was a long way from the Rhineland where this stoneware was made and demand always exceeded supply. The manufacture of glass bottles, long-necked and bulbous (the 'shaft and globe'), was well established by 1630. Many bottles made from the seventeenth century onwards bore a seal in the form of a circular raised medallion of glass impressed with a device, the most sought after showing name, place, and date, presumably the name being that of the wine merchant or the owner. The earliest surviving dated bottle was made in 1657. During the eighteenth century the shape gradually evolved into something like the modern claret bottle, with a short neck, high shoulders, and a more or less cylindrical body. One of the reasons for this evolution was the introduction of the cork at the end of the seventeenth century. This necessitated storing bottles in racks, on their sides, to keep the wine in contact with the cork, although there is reason to think that some were stored upside down. Early bottles had a ring of trailed glass round the neck just below the mouth, sometimes called a string rim. These were required before the flush cork came into general use, because early corks needed to be kept in place with string, in much the same way as the modern champagne cork is wired.

To prevent smuggling, the import of wine in bottles was forbidden in 1727 and the Act was not repealed till 1802. After this date the distinctive bottle shapes for Continental wines —those for claret, burgundy, hock, and champagne, for instance—were evolved, bottles for port and sherry remaining in the form then in use. The Roman idea of square-section bottles for easy storage was revived for gin bottles. These were termed *case* bottles, because they were intended to fit into wooden cases.

In the nineteenth century the demand for wine, and the various kinds of potable liquors, grew rapidly. Gin, the drink in England of the lowest class in the community, was kept in large ornamental stoneware bottles, and dispensed into smaller, decorative bottles moulded in the form of notabilities of the day, often with the name of the tavern impressed. Stoneware was probably employed as the cheapest kind of bottle, as well as the least vulnerable to accidental damage. The idea of moulding glass bottles, especially those for liquors, in similar decorative forms was probably French in origin, but American bottles were produced in a far greater variety of forms, many of them grotesque. The subject is vast, but this, and pressed glass generally, is examined in detail

by Albert Revi in his book, *American Pressed
Glass and Figure Bottles* (1969), which is the
definitive work on these subjects. American
bottles were not only made to contain all kinds
of wines and potable liquors, but also quack
medicines. A bottle in the form of a horse's hoof
held Mackay's Hoof Ointment, for instance,
one for poison was in the form of a coffin, and
another shaped like a human femur was
employed for the same purpose.

The bottle-making industry in England was
founded by Sir Robert Mansell, whose 'shaft
and globe' was made of a thick, coarse, dark
green glass, and bottle glass was often employed
thereafter for other purposes, such as the nineteenth-century doorstops. The colour of glass
of this type was not invariably green, and a dark
brown glass is often seen.

Large decorative bottles and flasks are not

very common survivals before the nineteenth century, but they can be found from most glassmaking centres in a variety of techniques. Small bottles intended for perfumes and similar purposes are much more numerous. The Egyptians, as already noted, made small vessels of this kind, and survivals from Roman days are almost common. Islamic glass includes small bottles of lapidary-carved glass in the manner of rock crystal, and the Venetians made perfume bottles and sprinklers for perfumed water, some of the best in *latticinio* glass. By the eighteenth century the variety was considerable. Not only were there decorative bottles for perfume and toilet waters, but cruet stands were provided with cut-glass oil and vinegar bottles and pepper and salt containers with silver sprinklers. Double flasks for oil and vinegar, the spouts inclining in opposite directions, came into use in the eighteenth century.

Small scent bottles made of Bristol white and coloured glasses were enamelled or gilded in characteristic style, and specimens exist (especially those decorated with exotic birds) which were obviously painted by James Giles in his Clerkenwell studio. The Chelsea porcelain factory, about this time (1755–65) was making scent bottles in large quantities and in a great variety of shapes that were difficult to make in glass. Some Bristol glass bottles bear a noteworthy resemblance to plain, flat Chelsea bottles, and it is possible that their manufacture may have been suggested to the Bristol glassmakers by Giles, who always found difficulty in procuring sufficient white porcelain to paint to supply his trade. Cut-glass scent and smelling bottles were commonly made in the second half of the eighteenth century, and in the nineteenth century Apsley Pellatt specialized in small wares of this kind, usually with cutting and sometimes with *crystallo-ceramie* additions. At the beginning of the twentieth century Art Nouveau scent bottles were made specially for Coty by Lalique, and for Guerlain by Baccarat. These, of excellent and novel designs, are now collected. Small bottles for purposes such as these were often mounted in gold and silver, or provided with stoppers of one or other of these metals like the flasks shown on page 71.

Opposite, above:
Flask of green glass moulded with the American eagle and masonic emblems. American, *c.* 1825. An early example of what was then a quite new technique. Masonic emblems occur on English and American glass from time to time.

Opposite, far right:
Opaline glass bottle, Bohemian, *c.* 1840. This bottle has been treated by the cutter as a semiprecious stone rather than as glass, because the material's inherent property of light refraction—enhanced by the facet cutting of crystal glass—is almost absent when it is opacified.

Opposite, below:
Press-moulded bottle with Pike's Peak in relief, unknown factory, probably American, mid-19th century. The words 'For Pike's Peak' are associated with the Colorado gold rush of 1858, and the miners' slogan 'Pike's Peak or bust'. These moulded bottles are now much prized by American collectors and many of them commemorate notable events of the period, as does this one.

Near left:
Oval flask with wheel-engraved decoration, including a coat of arms, Silesian, *c.* 1725. The arms are surrounded by *Bandwerk* (strapwork), a familiar type of Baroque ornament.

Far left:
Flask of a type associated with the Nailsea glassworks near Bristol, early 19th century.

Decanters, Claret jugs and Carafes

The earliest glass decanters date from the end of the seventeenth century, and their primary purpose was to act as containers into which wine was decanted from the cask for service at the table. The earliest vessels to be thus used in England were of Rhineland stoneware, first imported late in the sixteenth century. These were followed just before 1650 by vessels made of Lambeth delftware, many of which had the name of the wine, the date, and a characteristic decoration of the period painted on them. The later purpose of pouring wine from bottles into decanters was to retain sediment in the bottle, and, still later, wines such as port or sherry were decanted into vessels which were *en suite* with glasses and the remaining tableware.

Towards the end of the eighteenth century handsomely decorated cases were made complete with decanters of square section and glasses *en suite*, the decanters containing spirits and liqueurs. These 'squares' were introduced soon after 1750. They seem to have been a French innovation, and, like the travelling tea and coffee services of the period, were at first intended for travellers. In the nineteenth century cases became larger, heavier, and more elaborately decorated and were obviously intended for a more or less fixed place. They were provided with good locks to preserve the contents from the depredations of the staff. Where the decanters were visible but locked up, a spirit stand of this kind was often termed a *tantalus*, after the mythological Tantalus who was condemned to stand up to his neck in water without being allowed to drink.

Lead glass decanters were made by George Ravenscroft, at the end of the seventeenth century, and were intended to replace stoneware and delft bottles. Among the earliest specimens are the very rare bottle-decanters. An example in the Cecil Higgins collection at Bedford is illustrated on page 80. It has a cruciform body, and the shaft is ringed near the top in the manner of early wine-bottles. Early decanters were of better quality glass than bottles, and both quality and workmanship continued to improve with the passing of time. By the 1720's a mallet- or club-shaped form had made an appearance. It had a cone-shaped, or 'spire', glass stopper, which was uncut before 1750, and ornamented with cutting after that date.

Stoppers were introduced before 1750, but it is difficult to be sure at exactly what date.

By 1755 the practice of engraving the name of the contents within a formal border of vine leaves and grapes (label decanters) had started, but this proved inconvenient, since it limited the use of the decanter to the single wine on the label. The practice of making silver bottle tickets with chains to hang them round the neck of the decanter started at about this time, making an engraved label unnecessary.

By the 1750's decanters were being cut all over with shallow facets, at first flat, but later hollowed. Faceting became more pronounced soon after 1760, and the base was often cut with short vertical flutes. Soon after 1770 cutting was becoming general. An advertisement by Christopher Heady of Bath in 1775 referred to 'barrel-shaped decanters cut on an entirely new pattern' which probably meant the deeper cutting that was then beginning to replace the shallow faceting of the earlier specimens. From 1760 to 1770 the stopper was disc-shaped, the edges usually scalloped. Barrel-shaped decanters were supplied with a stopper of mushroom shape, and this remained standard for many years.

A word of caution is necessary here. Stoppers are easily lost and broken, and some antique decanters offered for sale have replacements. For this reason it is necessary to look carefully to be certain that the stopper is the right shape for the period, and that it matches the type of glass and its decoration. A well-matching stopper to a decanter intended for use matters little if the substitution is reflected in the price, but if the specimen is intended to take its place in a collection it needs the original stopper. Records exist of decanters being sent to Waterford to have stoppers matched to them. Even if this could be proved in a particular case, it would not affect the value of a specimen today.

The barrel-shaped decanter was a favourite with the Irish glassmakers, who decorated it in a variety of ways. Early Irish decanters are lightly decorated with engraving, and were given flattened, disc-shaped stoppers. A characteristic of Irish decanters is the presence of neck rings, which were first added to barrel-shaped decanters. It has been suggested that the purpose of these rings was to prevent a

heavy cut-glass decanter from slipping through the fingers. Because they are also found on earlier, much lighter decanters, however, this is a little doubtful. The rings vary from two to three.

Ships' decanters, often called Rodney decanters, are squat, with a very wide base, a ringed neck, and a mushroom stopper. The shape is a very practical one, intended for the service of wine during rough weather. They were termed Rodney decanters after Admiral Rodney, who defeated the French fleet off Cape St Vincent in 1780.

The Beilby family of glass enamellers painted decanters, some of which have survived. Decanters of both clear and coloured glass were decorated with enamelling, most of them coming from Bristol. Usually the gilding was simple, and confined to the name of the contents and a plain surrounding border, but a few rare specimens are more elaborately decorated with such motifs as exotic birds in gilt silhouette, in the manner of the London decorator James Giles, which were a fashionable decoration of around 1765 copied from Sèvres porcelain.

Coloured glass decanters were being made as early as 1820 at Stourbridge, and slightly later, slender examples flashed with ruby glass over clear glass and engraved with grapes and vine leaves were made, originally *en suite*, but now rarely accompanied by any of the other pieces.

At the end of the seventeenth century coloured glass decanters, not unlike the English 'shaft and globe' bottle, were being made in Germany, usually with enamelling, and with a handle and trailed decoration not found on English specimens. Decanters inspired by English styles were made in France towards the end of the eighteenth century, although cutting is always limited to light faceting.

Decanters were also made at La Granja de San Ildefonso in Spain. Some specimens are lightly

Left :
Cruciform decanter, English, early 18th century. This very rare decanter has an elongated neck and a ribbed collar near the top for tying on a cork with string.

Opposite, top left :
Large bell-shaped decanter, English, early 18th century.

Opposite, top right :
Ale decanter with facet-cut neck and target stopper, English, late 18th century. It was the custom to decant ale as well as wine in the 18th century, probably in order to clear it of sediment. Engraved specimens usually have the hop vine as ornament in place of the grape vine often found on wine decanters.

Opposite, below left :
Ship's decanter with a ringed neck, English, early 19th century. Broad-based so that it would slide rather than overturn when the table tilted, the ship's decanter, sometimes called a 'Rodney decanter' after Admiral Lord Rodney, victor of the Battle of Cape St Vincent, was a very practical vessel. The rings are intended to prevent the neck from slipping through the fingers.

Opposite, below right :
Cut-glass decanter by William Powell, Temple Gate, Bristol, early 19th century. Bristol was famous in the 18th century for the high quality of its cut glass.

Above :
Bottle-decanter of soda glass, decorated with trailing 'nipt diamond waies', English, *c.* 1665. Very little English glass has survived that is earlier than the last quarter of the 17th century, so this is a great rarity. The description of the manner in which the trailed decoration has been pincered to form diamond or lozenge shapes comes from George Ravenscroft's price list of 1677, and Ravenscroft made vessels similar to this one, but earlier use of this kind of decoration is evident from this decanter's existence. The origin of this work was Venetian. A plain wine jug similar in form to this one occurs in a 14th-century Bolognese fresco depicting a feast.

Right :
Pair of green glass label decanters in a papier-mâché stand, *c.* 1690. These excellent specimens of label decanters—which carry the name of their contents in a gilt label on the shoulder— also possess a contemporary stand of papier-mâché, which is very rare. Gilt labels are usually found on blue or green glass decanters, rarely on those made of clear glass, where the name of the contents is usually engraved. Decanters of this kind were produced by the firm of Isaac Jacobs of Temple Street, Bristol, glass manufacturers to George III. The labelling may have been done by Michael Edkins (*fl.* 1760– 1790), who painted both faïence and glass.

cut and finely decorated with gilt ornament, while a later type, of barrel shape with neck rings, was decorated in bright enamel colours. The *pórron*, a wine vessel with a large tubular spout for filling and a smaller spout for pouring, must certainly be classified as a decanter, and this is a traditional Spanish type which is still being made in its simpler forms.

Decanters were not manufactured in large quantities in America, and nineteenth-century catalogues of glassware rarely show specimens. The New England Glass Company made decorative bottles for cologne and toilet water, and a limited number of decanters, but it must be assumed that most were imported from Ireland. The manufacture of pressed glass decanters posed some problems, and was probably uneconomic.

Claret or wine jugs with handles and stoppers date from the end of the seventeenth century. They were made in most European countries, and vary widely in shape. The tall, straight-sided, tapering jugs with silver mounts and decorative cutting were popular in Victorian England, and continued to be made into the twentieth century. Decorative wine jugs were also made by such artists as Emile Gallé.

The carafe also belongs to this category. It is a bottle without a stopper, intended for wine or water. It lacks a stopper because a tumbler could be inverted over the mouth to rest on the shoulders. Carafes were first made in England after about 1750, when they were termed *water crafts*. Decoration is usually engraved, but trailing was sometimes employed as simple ornament. Until about 1800 carafes were put on the dining table, but in England they were thereafter relegated to the bedroom. They have recently come back into fashion and are employed to serve wine that is drawn directly from the cask which is known as *vin en carafe*.

Right, above :
Decanter jug with wheel engraving from La Granja de San Ildefonso, Spain, mid-18th century.

Right, below :
Decanter engraved with Jacobite symbols, English, *c*. 1750. The engraving may possibly be later. Because Jacobite sympathies in the 18th century were treasonable and adherents to the Stuart cause were persecuted from time to time according to the political climate, it is obvious that many glasses were bought in a plain state and given to someone regarded as reliable for decoration. It is doubtful whether any established glasshouse would have felt safe in producing glasses thus decorated for general use, except, possibly, in Scotland or the north of England.

Opposite :
Crystal jug etched with the subject of two monks enjoying a joke, Stourbridge, *c*. 1860. The middle of the 19th century saw a revival of interest in the Middle Ages and medieval styles were popular for the decoration of materials of all kinds. Paintings of monks and cardinals carousing were common, and this subject may have been derived from an actual painting or engraving of this kind. The decoration of this jug has been etched with the aid of hydrofluoric acid, and it is rare to find anything so elaborate done in this way. The technique was usually limited to simple ornament, or to the removal of unwanted glass in cameo cutting.

Bowls and Tableservices

Centrepiece for a table decoration, Venice, 18th century. Centrepieces like this are very rare today. In the 18th century they were the focus of a table decoration with a single unifying theme to which all the parts conformed. This garden with fountains may have been accompanied by glass figures dotted about among the table appointments.

Bowls are a very common survival. They are a useful type of vessel for many purposes, and obviously were always made in great variety. In eighteenth-century English glass, for instance, it is possible to recognize punch bowls, salad bowls, sugar bowls, butter bowls, sweetmeat bowls, finger bowls, bowls for salt, and even goldfish bowls. This is not an exhaustive list; it merely provides a guide to the scope of the subject. Bowls were designed to stand directly on the table, or were provided with pedestal bases. They were decorated with cutting, wheel engraving, diamond engraving, enamelling, simple trailing, or trailing 'nipt diamond waies'. They can be found in coloured, flashed, or cased glass, with or without wheel engraving. Bowls may be circular or oval, the latter especially favoured by Irish glassmakers in conjunction with a heavy pedestal foot and elaborately cut decoration. They range from large (sometimes very large) punch bowls to small salts.

The large fruit and salad bowls were set in the centre of the table, and were, in some cases, part of a set of table glass which included water jugs, decanters, claret jugs, wineglasses, and tumblers decorated *en suite*, usually with cutting or engraving, but it is very rare to find a reasonably complete set today, although nineteenth-century sets of table glass reduced to perhaps half the original number have sometimes survived.

Comparatively rare are glass services of the type usually made in porcelain or earthenware, although a comport, plate, and candlestick from an almost complete dessert service made by Sowerby of Gateshead in 1870 are shown on page 92. The eighteenth-century Venetian plate of opaque white glass with a view of San Giorgio Maggiore (page 88) is part of a service of 24 such plates brought back to England from Venice by Horace Walpole in 1741. These were obviously based on contemporary porcelain. The tea bowl and saucer painted in the Metzsch workshop at Bayreuth about 1750 (page 88) must have been part of a tea service also based on contemporary porcelain. Sugar bowls, cream jugs, and slop bowls of *Milchglas* are known from Basdorf.

Great attention was paid in seventeenth- and eighteenth-century Europe to the art of elaborate table decoration. Most such decorations had a theme of one kind or another, which was carried out in the seventeenth century with figures and small models of wax or sugar. In the eighteenth century porcelain replaced these early materials, and a large centrepiece in a variety of forms (one Meissen example being a classical temple built up of numerous parts) would be surrounded by porcelain figures contributing to the main theme, with service ware *en suite*. The small porcelain figures made fashionable by Meissen in the 1730's were always part of a table decoration, and also always part of a set. An early example is the famous Meissen 'Swan' service with water as its theme, and an accompanying decoration of swans, nereids, tritons, and so forth.

These decorations must have been very rare in glass at the time, because little has survived to indicate that they were commonly made in this material, but an elaborate centrepiece is preserved in the Museo Vetrario, Murano, in the form of a miniature garden, with a central architectural fountain which was 'water' made out of spun glass, columns topped with urns, miniature balustrades, and pots with flowering plants made of glass (opposite). Belonging to the same category are the rare Venetian stands with glass fruits, and figures of glass, such as those of Moors, made 'at the lamp'. All were intended for table decoration, and all were once probably part of a set, or series. It is likely that some of the surviving free-standing glass figures from Nevers (especially those of the eighteenth century such as those on page 38), which resembled porcelain figures in size and design were intended originally as table decoration, and contributed to some kind of central theme. It is, perhaps, some indication of the scope and complexity of these decorations that dessert courses were often taken at a separate table, to which the guests moved. This was provided with a different decoration from that at which the earlier courses were served. In the case of porcelain, Meissen figures marked *KHC* for Königliche Hof Conditorei—'royal court confectionary' or *KHK* for Königliche Hof Küche—'royal court kitchen', are far from unknown. The now rare Saxon enamelled glasses termed *Hof Kellerei* (court cellar) glasses belong to a similar category.

Left, top :
Plate of porcelain form in
opaque white glass enamelled
with a view of San Giorgio
Maggiore, Venice, mid-18th
century. Formerly in Horace
Walpole's collection at
Strawberry Hill. In a letter
dated 1743 the Countess of
Hertford wrote: 'The difference between old china and
glassware is not in the trans-
parency... but a bluish cast in
the white only observable
when placed by real china.'

Left, centre, and bottom :
Tea bowl and saucer imitating
porcelain, from the studio of
Hausmaler Metzsch,
Bayreuth, *c.* 1745.

Above :
Cup plate of press-moulded
blue glass, probably from
Sandwich, Massachusetts,
c. 1835. Cup plates in a wide
variety of moulded patterns
are a favourite collectors'
item.

This fashion hardly survived the eighteenth
century, although vast silver centrepieces and
accompanying table decorations *en suite* continued to be made in the early decades of the
nineteenth century, perhaps the finest known
being the 'Portuguese' service, which was
presented to the Duke of Wellington and is
now at Apsley House, London.

Although silver was sometimes employed
for the service of wine, and pewter and silver
for that of ale, porcelain was hardly ever used
for either of these purposes, and porcelain
dinner and dessert services were complemented
by wineglasses, and by such vessels as decanters.
This line of demarcation was nearly always
observed, for examples of either material stray-
ing into the preserves of the other are comparatively rare. Of the two, the glass manufacturers
were sometimes tempted by the possiblity of
expanding their market to make glass in imitation of porcelain, but the methods of manufacture of the two materials are so far apart that
neither could imitate the other successfully.

Opposite, above :
Oval fruit bowl decorated
with festoons and shell motifs,
Irish, *c.* 1800. The oval cut-
glass bowl is nearly always
Irish. Most of them are boat-
shaped, higher at either end
than in the middle. Bowls of
this kind were usually
decorated more ambitiously
than most other wares, and the
shell is an uncommon motif.

Opposite, below :
Butter cooler with cover with
flat cutting, Irish, *c.* 1800.
Glass is peculiarly suitable as
a container for butter because
it is cool and the contents can
be seen. Objects of domestic
use such as this, however,
have rarely survived, because
the covers have almost
invariably been broken.

Above, left :
Covered butter dish of opal glass simulating alabaster with knop and snake of green glass and added gilt ornament, Stourbridge, last quarter of the 19th century. The snake is a not infrequent ornament on Stourbridge glass of this period. The combination of colours here is particularly harmonious and the form simple and restrained.

Above, right :
Bowl of amethyst glass with gilded flat-relief frieze, Bohemia, *c.* 1890, signed in diamond point *Moser, Karlsbad.* Ludwig Moser (1833–1916) learned the art of glass engraving as a pupil of Andreas Mattoni and founded his own firm near Karlsbad in 1857. A recent Continental handbook states that signed examples of his work are unknown, so this bowl must be a considerable rarity.

Below, left :
Cranberry glass bowl, Stourbridge, *c.* 1870. Cranberry glass is the name given by American collectors to the rose-pink table glass made especially at Stourbridge in huge quantities in the second half of the 19th century. Wine-glasses are the commonest survival, but jugs, carafes, decanters, tumblers and many other domestic wares still exist. More elaborate wares requiring craftsmanship of a higher order were also made, often decorated with glass threading, usually of clear glass, added by a machine patented by Richardson of Stourbridge. Ornament was also trailed and pincered, and cut and engraved ornament sometimes occurs on objects of clear glass 'flashed' (i.e., having a very thin surface layer) with cranberry glass.

Below, right :
Large cup of opal glass with crystal handle and foot decorated with ruby threading, Stourbridge, *c.* 1875. An unusual treatment of the decoration in which threading is utilized to form geometric patterns.

Glass plates became popular in America with the development of pressed glass, especially those made of lacy glass, and the small cup plate shown on page 88 was made as an adjunct to the cups and saucers of porcelain. It was fashionable to pour tea into a deep saucer and to drink it from this, and the cup plate provided a place on which to stand the cup while the tea was being consumed.

Covered comports, like the one illustrated on page 93, were used for a variety of purposes. Covered butter dishes, cruet bottles, salt cellars, pepper shakers, toothpick glasses, candy trays, celery stands, custard cups, spoon holders, pickle dishes, relish dishes, cream jugs, preserve jars, and sauceboats are examples of the many objects available in conventional or novel forms. To judge from surviving catalogues, these were available *en suite* as a set, or could be purchased singly, thus providing for the replacement of breakages. In England however, services never became standardized in the same way as porcelain services, nor did it ever become the practice to make specially decorated services to order, a practice the major European porcelain factories still maintain.

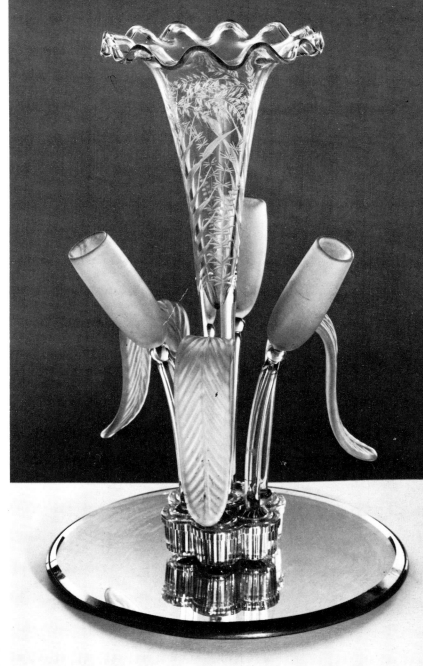

Opposite, above :
Plate and comport from a moulded opaque glass dessert service, and a table candle-stick from a set of four, by J. C. Sowerby & Co., Gateshead-on-Tyne, with peacock's head mark, 1876. Sowerby produced a great deal of moulded glass during the second half of the 19th century, much of it in competition with the porcelain factories. Unlike earlier makers, however, Sowerby did not attempt to imitate the appearance and decoration of porcelain.

Opposite, below :
Cruet bottles and boat-shaped stand in the Adam style, the bottles with silver mounts, English, *c.* 1780. Complete 18th-century cruet sets, such as this, are understandably extremely rare.

Above, left :
Covered comport of press-moulded glass by William T. Gillinder, Philadelphia, *c.* 1870.

Above, right :
Centrepiece for the dining table, probably Stourbridge, *c.* 1875.

Below, right :
Two-handled stand for cruet set, French, 18th century. The word *cruet,* originally French, means a small glass bottle for vinegar or oil for the dining table, but it has been extended to include containers for salt and pepper *en suite.*

Candlesticks, Candelabra and Chandeliers

Mosque lamp of enamelled glass decorated in *neskhi* script with a verse from the Koran and a dedicatory inscription for an emir who died in 1345, Syrian, *c.* 1330. The shield of arms, an eagle above a gold cup on a red ground, is an example of an Islamic heraldic device, a custom adopted by the Crusaders.

It is difficult to say when the first lighting appliances of glass were made. The Romans used pottery oil lamps for interior illumination, and although glass was probably employed for the same purpose, examples do not seem to have survived. Some of the finest specimens of Islamic enamelled glass are the mosque lamps of the mid-fourteenth century one of which is shown opposite. These are actually lamp containers, and were either set in a niche or suspended from the ceiling, usually the latter. The Koran refers to glass lamps thus: '... his [God's] light is as a niche in which is a lamp, and the lamp in a glass, the glass as it were a glittering star'. The interior lamp may have been of metal, pottery, or even a glass bowl of oil with a floating wick. Lamps were made in Venice for export to the East at the end of the sixteenth century.

There were no glass candlesticks before the invention of the candle of standard size. Before this date the metal pricket-candlestick, where the candle is impaled on a spike, was invariable. The candle nozzle, which was able to take a much smaller candle of standard size belongs to the beginning of the seventeenth century, but the candlestick of glass seems not to be evident any earlier than 1685. The drip pan on either silver or glass candlesticks was not added until much later.

The chandelier with cut faceted pendant drops was originally of rock crystal on a metal framework, and the superb chandeliers of the Galerie des Glaces at Versailles are of this kind. They continued to be made well into the eighteenth century, especially in France, but the lead glass of Ravenscroft provided an effective substitute for rock crystal, and in England the first chandeliers of this type, although they no longer exist, may have pre-dated 1700. The earliest reference to 'Glass Schandeliers' occurs in the *London Gazette* in 1714. The first mention of the term *lustres* applied to the pendant drops only occurs in 1728, and the term was later applied to the chandelier itself.

Candelabra—multibranched table candlesticks—first occur in metal in the seventeenth century with the introduction of the standard candle. The earliest plain glass specimens in England date from the beginning of the eighteenth century, and those that were additionally ornamented with pendant drops from about 1750. Branched candlesticks of this type were first termed *girandoles*, and sometimes lustres, the term *candelabra* only coming into general use early in the nineteenth century.

Early glass candlesticks, chandeliers, and candelabra are usually English, inspired by the particular suitability of Ravenscroft's lead glass for this purpose. Candlesticks and candelabra on the Continent are usually made of metal—brass, silver, or gilt-bronze—no doubt because of a more advanced metal industry, especially in France.

The first English candlesticks had hollow knopped stems and pedestal feet. They lacked a drip pan. Obviously they suffered from the disadvantage of being easily knocked over. This type was soon replaced by solid knopped stems on heavier bases which resembled the silver candlesticks of the period, a design that was not only safer but gave the glass more chance to exhibit its natural brilliance. The construction of candlesticks began to have something in common with wineglasses, themselves based on silver prototypes, the stems being of baluster form or with flattened annular knops. About 1715, with the advent of the Hanoverian George I, the Silesian stem was introduced for wine- and sweetmeat glasses, and for candlestick stems. Unlike the baluster stem, the Silesian stem was moulded with from four to eight ribs stemming from the high shoulder. A German version occurs as part of the Silesian *Pokal* illustrated on page 60. The earliest facet cutting in the making of candlesticks is recorded in 1742, and air-twist stems (see page 97) first appear about the same time. Opaque white twists occur, but specimens are very rare. Candlesticks of opaque white glass decorated with enamelled flowers were made in Bristol about the middle of the century.

With the advent of Adam and Neoclassicism the candlestick occasionally assumed the form of a classical column on a square, stepped base (no doubt copied from some contemporary silver candlesticks in this form), or that of an urn, a form employed by Irish glasshouses. Urns in a variety of materials, usually mounted in metal, commonly have a candle nozzle on the cover, the latter sometimes being reversible, the nozzle being turned inwards during the daytime.

Above, left :
Candlestick with an early
variety of air-twist stem,
containing air bubbles, and a
domed and terraced foot,
English, first quarter of the
18th century.

Above, right :
Candlestick with knopped
stem, air bubbles, and a
domed and terraced foot,
English, first quarter of the
18th century.

Below, left :
Cut-glass candlestick with
faceted stem, Irish, end of the
18th century. The Irish
glasshouses specialized in
candlesticks, usually with
heavy bases to prevent them
from being overturned.
Candleholders were often
removable to make them
easier to clean.

Below, centre :
Unusual taperstick with an
inverted funnel-shaped base
and faceted stem decorated
with light cutting, English,
mid-18th century.

Below, right :
Lacemaker's glass, French,
18th century. Filled with
water, this made a useful
magnifier for work by
artificial light.

Opposite, above :
Large candlestick of ribbed
glass with knopped stem and
high domed foot, English,
mid-18th century. Glass
candlesticks, because of their
light refraction, were always
a popular form of domestic
lighting.

Opposite, below :
Reading lamp for oil,
enamelled with Saxon arms,
dated 1677. The German
passion for dating everything
is extremely useful to the
glass historian.

The actual candle nozzles for glass candlesticks were, like their silver counterparts, often removable to facilitate replacing a burnt-out candle, and these became essential with the introduction of candlesticks hung with faceted drops, which were introduced towards the end of the eighteenth century. About this time candlesticks began to be made of a combination of various materials in imitation of the prevailing mode in France, where combinations of gilt-bronze and Sèvres porcelain were being employed as clock cases and candlesticks. About 1780 Wedgwood began to make drum-shaped bases of jasper stoneware which were mounted in ormolu, and surmounted by a glass candle nozzle, a drip pan hung with pendant drops, and a glass or ormulu stem.

Allied to the candlestick is a miniature version made for candles of a much smaller diameter, often called a taperstick. In the eighteenth century they were sometimes referred to as tea candlesticks, whence it has been conjectured that they illuminated the small drawing-room tea table. It is possible that they held a wax candle from which the inferior and much less expensive tallow candles were ignited. Certainly they formed part of the equipment of the writing desk, where they were employed to melt sealing wax. The silver or porcelain ink stand was usually given a recess for a taperstick, and tapersticks are also known in these materials.

The first candelabra hardly predate the middle of the eighteenth century, although rare examples of plain, branched candlesticks which could be thus classified have survived from still earlier periods. These, too, were often based on silver patterns. 'Glass lustres or girandoles' are recorded in 1753, and the term *candelabrum* came into use shortly before 1800. Essentially the candelabrum has at least two branches bearing candle nozzles, and sometimes four or more; only the earliest specimens are not decorated with cutting, and almost all are hung with faceted drops. From about 1770 to the end of the century the candelabrum had a greatly lengthened central stem hung with pendant drops at the top, the nozzles being carried on curving branches which sprang from the stem about one third of the way up. The faceting of the drops became increasingly elaborate as time passed, and, because they eventually concealed the arms, before the end of the century these were no longer being faceted. With the end of the Regency period glass candelabra became less fashionable, but they continued to be made throughout the nineteenth century. Normal glass candelabra vary from one to two feet in height, but seen at the Great Exhibition of 1851 was a pair eight feet high, made by Osler of Birmingham for the Queen, which must surely rank with Gracie Fields' aspidistra.

Chandeliers hung with faceted drops were first made in the seventeenth century, but the

Above left :
Lotus chandelier from the Music Room, Brighton Pavilion, 1817. The chandelier hangs from a great palmlike ornament in the centre of the ceiling in the form of a glass lustre. This, with its chains, acts as a suspensory point for the immense shade in the form of a lotus flower, its leaves decorated with Chinese figures. Underneath are flying dragons in gilt metal. Designed by Robert Jones, it was made by Parker & Perry (who also made the chandeliers in Buckingham Palace). Princess Lieven, wife of the Russian ambassador, wrote in a letter to Prince Metternich : 'I do not believe since the days of Heliogabalus there has been such magnificence and such luxury.'

Below, left :
Chandelier decorated with coloured floral and foliate ornament, from the Cà Rezzonico, Venice, probably by Giuseppe Briati, Murano, Venice, 18th century. Venetian soda glass was unsuitable for the facet cutting which decorated the pendant drops of Bohemian and English work, but made superb chandeliers like this one, in which floral and foliate ornament of coloured and clear glass was carried by a metal framework. Most such work was done in the 18th century, when the market for the more characteristic types of Venetian glass was flagging and novelties were being tried in an effort to revive it.

Opposite :
Rhododendron lamp of stained glass and bronze, Tiffany & Co., New York, *c.* 1908. Decorative lamps were among the most fashionable features of the Art Nouveau interior and were made in a variety of materials, from glass to bronze. The development of electric lighting in the 1880's encouraged the fashion. The best glass shades were made by Tiffany and Gallé, and this characteristic Tiffany example is among the best of its kind.

drops were of rock crystal, cut by Bohemian lapidaries. Chandeliers from Venice of the same period were built up of glass flowers, leaves, and fruits made 'at the lamp', and, since Venetian glass did not lend itself to cutting, any needful ornament of this kind was made from rock crystal. An exceptionally fine specimen is pictured on page 98.

'Schandeliers' in England may have been made before 1700, but they were not advertised till 1714, when they appeared under this name. The earliest chandeliers may not have been hung with drops, although there were a number of Continental precedents for this design dating back at least to 1670. One English chandelier dating from about 1732 is no more than a copy of a brass fixture of the period and this is probably the earliest example surviving. Throughout the remainder of the eighteenth century a type prevailed with faceted shafts, arms, nozzles, and drip pans, but hung with relatively few drops. Vast chandeliers, like those of the great houses of France, which had a pulley-like arrangement to enable them to be let down from the ceiling for cleaning, rarely occurred in England. Nor, so far as the records go, is it possible to trace the existence of the French custom of hiring large chandeliers from dealers for state occasions. Perhaps the finest eighteenth-century chandeliers in England are the 48-light examples that were made about 1770 to illuminate the Assembly Rooms of Bath. Worthy, also, to be ranked with some of the more imposing French chandeliers is the

central example in the Throne Room of Buckingham Palace, which was supplied by Perry and Company in 1835. Modern chandeliers of this type are now obtainable, and old ones usually need careful examination to be sure that the drops match reasonably well. As the late W. B. Honey once remarked, some of them are a miniature history of glass over the last 150 years.

Oil lamps date back to remote antiquity, but they were not widely used in England till about 1770. A Swiss named Argaud invented a close approach to the modern oil lamp, with an adjustable wick and a glass chimney, in or about 1770. It burned either colza oil (a vegetable oil made from rapeseed) or whale oil. Kerosene (paraffin oil) came into general use in the 1860's. During the second half of the nineteenth century ornamental lamps with glass oil reservoirs and outer decorated shades became increasingly popular. Outer shades were often made of opaline or cased glass, the latter characteristically treated by cutting through the outer layer with decorative designs.

The Art Nouveau period is notable for lamp shades of high quality made by Gallé, Daum Frères, Tiffany, and others, perhaps the most sought after currently being the mushroom-like shades by Tiffany. But the increasing use of electricity in the first decades of the twentieth century, by removing the risk of fire, made possible the use of fabrics, or even paper, in the making of shades, with the consequent decline of shades made from glass and porcelain.

Vases

Pair of small blue glass vases decorated with gilt traceries and opaque white glass panels painted with exotic birds in imitation of porcelain, Stourbridge, *c.* 1840. These vases are closely copied from slightly earlier Derby porcelain vases. The exotic birds, somewhat in the manner of the Sèvres bird painters, Evans and Aloncle, are particularly associated with porcelain painting.

The Oxford English Dictionary defines a vase as 'a vessel primarily intended for decorative purposes'. In this sense the vase is barely 200 years old. Chinese porcelain vases, and those of Greek pottery, however useless as objects of utility to later centuries, began their lives as vessels of practical worth. The first European vases were made of porcelain at Meissen at the beginning of the eighteenth century in imitation of those manufactured in the Orient. The Rococo period of the mid-eighteenth century is noted for its love of flowers and many flower and plant holders of all kinds were made out of Sèvres porcelain. The Neoclassical period which followed brought copies of Greek pottery forms in both earthenware and porcelain.

The earliest glass vases were small and came from Venice in the sixteenth century. They are usually termed *bouquetières* (a word which actually means 'flower-girl'), and were used to hold cut flowers. Looking rather like a large wine goblet with an elaborately convoluted stem, they were purely decorative in intent, and not very practical for their purpose. In mid-eighteenth-century England the Bristol glasshouses were making small copies of Chinese vases in glass opacified with tin oxide in the same manner as the Bristol delft glaze, and enamelled with Chinese figures, or European flowers inspired by the naturally depicted German flowers (*Deutsche Blumen*) to be found on contemporary Meissen and Chelsea porcelain. Work of this kind can be regarded as a porcelain substitute. In the later glass of the eighteenth century the tall cylindrical cut-glass vessel on a short stem and spreading foot, slightly flared at the rim (some of them from Cork or Dublin), are not flower vases—although they are often used for this purpose today—but celery glasses.

The earliest true vases, as the term is now employed, belong to the first decades of the nineteenth century, and these were made of opaline glass. Vases of this kind occurred in France as early as 1810, and their forms were much influenced by the prevailing Empire style. Although many other decorative objects of domestic utility were made of opaline, the vase in a variety of colours seems to have predominated. Vases were decorated in both cold colours and enamels, and the former type is usually referable to a date before 1835.

Vases of opaline glass which were based on Greek pottery, often with more than a side glance at Chinese porcelain forms in addition, and decorated with classical motifs in enamels, were shown at the 1851 Great Exhibition in London by Richardson of Stourbridge, for which they were awarded a prize medal. What were termed *flower-glasses*, intended for metal mounts, were being made at Stourbridge, according to the records, as early as 1842, but identifiable specimens do not seem to have survived. Richardson also made vases of a slim and elegant form imitating Bohemian work and decorated in the revived Rococo style.

The revival of cameo cutting by John Northwood led to the manufacture of vases which, for practical purposes, were too costly to put anywhere but in a cabinet. The Northwood copy of the Portland Vase cost 1,000 gold pounds to make, the equivalent of about £10,000 or $25,000 (1973). Some of the cameo-cut vases made by Northwood's followers owe much in their form to more or less contemporary Chinese porcelain imports. Others are directly influenced by the Japanese art which had started to reach Europe after 1853, the year in which Commodore Perry of the United States Navy sailed into Nagasaki harbour with four ships of war to open diplomatic relations with the outside world. Japanese art at once made a considerable impact on Europe. It had not been generally known and admired since a brief period early in the eighteenth century, at which time its porcelain was widely sought and imitated. Soon wood-block prints, fans, fabrics, furniture, and metalwork were being imported in large quantities, and not only influenced the work of porcelain factories such as Worcester in the 1870's, but such painters as Manet, Monet, Degas, Whistler and Van Gogh, and glassworkers such as Eugène Rousseau and Gallé (page 119). At the same time the Japanese concept of an object intended only as decoration—the *okimono*, or ornamental object for a special place such as a niche or alcove—reached Europe, and vases began to be made which were decorative in their own right, and not intended for flowers.

The asymmetry of Japanese art, and its floral subjects, also made a considerable contribution

to the Art Nouveau style of the 1890's, when vase forms variously decorated were popular with European glassmakers, and in modern times vases have continued to be made by all the major centres that produce artistic glass.

Bottle and flask shapes not intended for practical use are often classed as vases. The silver-mounted glass flasks by Carl Fabergé, shown on page 71, are probably an example of this category. They are unusual, since Fabergé nearly always employed rock crystal or hardstones for his smaller work. No doubt glass was employed in this case because of the large size of the flasks.

Vases of variable quality decorated in a number of ways were hung with faceted drops of crystal glass pendant from the rim. These are usually termed *vases lustres*, and developed in the nineteenth century from the candlestick and candelabrum thus decorated. The best vase lustres came from Bohemia, and were made of opaque glass cased over clear white, or coloured crystal. Similar work was also produced at Stourbridge. Some are fitted with a brass candle holder in the interior.

Mention has been made of some of the techniques employed for the making and decorating of vases, but almost every process known to the glassmaker has been employed for this purpose in the past two centuries. Although earlier forms owed much to porcelain—and some vases were literally no more than frank imitations of this substance (see pages 41, 42 and 47)—from the time of Gallé onwards increasing use has been made of the ductile properties of glass, and modern vases bear no relation at all to porcelain.

see pages 41, 42 and 47

Left, above:
Vase of opaque white glass decorated in brown enamel with figures in the 'Etruscan' style, George Bacchus & Sons, marked 'Vitrified enamel colours, Birmingham', *c.* 1850. Transfer printing, an English invention in the mid-18th century, had been extensively employed since that time for decorating both pottery and porcelain. There was no technical reason why it should not have been applied to glass decoration, but Bacchus seem to have been the first to do it. Similar vases, however, were produced about the same time by Richardson of Stourbridge.

Left, below:
Vase of amber-coloured glass with floral decoration in relief, signed Emile Gallé, Nancy, late 19th century. Much of Gallé's work is in the form of decorative vases such as this.

Left, centre:
Large *bouquetière* of deep blue glass with diamond engraving and traces of gilding, probably Hall-in-the-Tirol, second half of the 16th century. The form appears to be based on the Spanish *almorrata* (rose-water sprinkler), also made at Venice. The diamond engraving of Hall, inspired by that of the Venetians, was executed on blue, green and crystal glass. Oil gilding was sometimes added, but this has usually rubbed off over the years. Engravers from Hall emigrated to Vienna and Nürnberg, taking their art with them.

Opposite:
Celery glass decorated with heavy cutting, English, *c.* 1830. Often mistaken for a flower vase—and quite capable of serving that purpose—is the celery glass. It is first to be seen late in the 18th century, made with a short stem and spreading foot. Some Irish specimens from Cork and Dublin have a square foot, and were given a wide turned-over rim like the salad bowls of the period.

Paperweights

The first objects of glass expressly made as paperweights were a nineteenth-century innovation. Early in the seventeenth century small bronzes had been designed for this purpose, and reclining *putti* of porcelain were mounted in gilt-bronze as *presse-papiers* in mid-eighteenth-century France. The technique of enclosing a small cameo of porcelain, or some similar material, in a ball of glass (variously known as *crystallo-ceramies*, sulphides, and incrustations) may well have begun in Bohemia about the middle of the eighteenth century, but it was first developed at the end of that century by a French glassworker named Barthélemy Deprez, and a patent was taken out by the English glassmaker, Apsley Pellatt, in 1819. This process was not limited to paperweights, but was used to decorate a variety of objects, especially decanters.

The paperweights which are most sought by collectors at present are also among the most colourful objects to be made from glass, and are often technically the most ingenious. Those widely sought are principally of the *millefiori* type, a technique that was briefly described in Chapter I. The term *millefiori* means 'thousand flowers', which is not to be taken literally. It is generally regarded as having been coined in Venice in the nineteenth century, but it was current in eighteenth-century France as *mille-fleurs* to describe the porcelain vases from China and Meissen which were entirely covered with small painted or modelled flowers. In glass the term refers to numerous flower-like sections of multicoloured canes arranged in a close pattern which, especially in the case of paperweights, are embedded in clear glass. The technique was first devised in Alexandria in the first century AD for making bowls and dishes. The words of Sabellico at the end of the fifteenth century have already been quoted, but it is uncertain whether he was referring to a *millefiori* paperweight as the term is now understood; if he was, no specimen has survived, and no other reference exists to similar work at this time. The earliest Venetian paperweights of which we can be certain are a combination of *latticinio* and *millefiori* work made just before 1845 by Pierre Bigaglia.

By this year the technique was also being employed by the French factory of Saint-Louis, and the earliest dated weight from here is actually 1845, although the dates most commonly seen are 1847 and 1848, with 1849 as the latest. Baccarat made similar weights dated from 1846 to 1849, the commonest year being 1848. Clichy weights are not dated, but some have the letter *C* in the decoration, and the name is spelled out in a few rare instances. The finest quality weights usually come from Saint-Louis, and those of Baccarat are the scarcest. Decorated with similar techniques are such small objects as ornamental inkwells, perfume bottles, vases and drinking glasses, doorknobs, *tazza*s (shallow bowls set on pedestals), decanters, and seals. Although paperweights of this kind were widely made elsewhere, by common consent the finest came from these three French factories, and were made from 1845 to 1850. Manufacture continued after the latter year, but the vogue was declining, and competition from elsewhere was becoming keener. Large sums are now paid for the best and the rarest, and because of the technique of manufacture, no two weights are ever precisely alike. The dates are part of the pattern, and are often difficult to find unless the weight is carefully inspected.

Great ingenuity was displayed in selecting and arranging the glass rods which, when fused, were drawn out into canes. Those of special shapes were made with the aid of metal moulds and cased with clear glass before being drawn out, the casing preserving the shape. Sections were cut from a variety of canes and arranged in a shallow circular mould which was heated to fuse them together. The mass was then withdrawn on the pontil rod and repeatedly immersed in a pot of molten clear glass till it had acquired the requisite size and shape. In some rare instances, as in the specimens from Saint-Louis opposite, the weight was cased with opaque glass (overlay weights), and this layer was then ground through to the clear glass beneath, providing 'windows' through which the interior *millefiori* work could be seen.

Although *millefiori* weights are the commonest, the decoration takes many other forms which are too numerous to attempt to list here. For detailed information the reader is referred to Paul Hollister's *Encyclopedia of Glass Paperweights* (1969), which is the most comprehensive

work on this subject. Flower weights are those which employ natural flowers as decoration, either large single flowers, or garlands and small bouquets. Pansies, primroses, and clematis are the commonest, but a variety of flowers is represented in this way. The rose is probably the rarest, and the dahlia is much sought after. Weights featuring fruit and vegetables come more frequently from Saint-Louis.

Butterflies, either alone or accompanying a flower, occur among the weights from Baccarat, as well as the much rarer specimens which depict a caterpillar. More common than the latter are weights depicting a snake coiled on grounds of various colours, or a salamander, both of which come from Baccarat and Saint-Louis. Saint-Louis weights often feature miniature silhouettes of animals such as the dog, horse, or bird, which sometimes form a central motif surrounded by *millefiori* canes.

The 'ground' of a paperweight is a coloured close pattern on which the principal design is superimposed. Carpet grounds are those formed from closely packed miniature canes, and these are often greatly prized. *Latticinio* work sometimes occurs in conjunction with carpet grounds at Baccarat and Clichy. *Latticinio* work looking like twisted gauze floating in the glass is found with some Clichy weights, and is sometimes called a muslin ground. An irregular, sandy-looking ground accompanies snakes and lizards.

Most French weights are about three inches in diameter. Miniatures are about two inches, and magnums about four inches in diameter. Most miniature weights come from Clichy; they are somewhat less common from Baccarat or Saint-Louis. Magnums are rare from any of these factories, and most weights of from three-and-a-half to four inches, or even larger are English, from Stourbridge, where the earliest specimens seem to have been made in or about 1845, the technique probably introduced from France by Apsley Pellatt, who was always alert for novelties. It is possible that paperweight manufacture in England was established with the aid of workmen from Clichy. There is a kind of family resemblance between some Stourbridge weights and those from Clichy, except that the decorative elements of the former are larger, coarser, and less brilliant in colour. Stourbridge also imitated such Clichy products as *millefiori* inkwells and rulers.

In 1848 paperweights were being made by George Bacchus and Sons of Birmingham and the technique was described in a contemporary journal as coming from Bohemia, whose work was giving considerable inspiration to Bacchus at the time. Bohemian factories were certainly experimenting with *latticinio* and *millefiori* about this time in the course of attempts to revive Venetian styles generally. Although the only dated Bohemian paperweight was made in 1848, it is obvious from the quality that the first weights must have been made several years earlier. The question often is, Who was copying

whom? French and Bohemian weights frequently have decorative motifs in common, especially those of Baccarat, but French weights are of lead glass instead of potash glass, and are heavier and more brilliant in consequence.

In separating weights the origin of which is doubtful there is a chemical spot test for the presence of lead. This is sometimes employed for the same purpose in the case of some early porcelains which have massive quantities of lead in the body. Carefully carried out, it does not damage a specimen. In recent times the ultraviolet lamp has been employed to attribute French weights. When ultraviolet light is used to illuminate certain substances, visible light of one of a variety of colours, the colour depending on the nature of the substance, is reflected. This phenomenon is known as fluorescence. Examination of French weights in this way has shown that Baccarat weights usually fluoresce with a deep blue, Saint-Louis with a peachy pink, and Clichy with lime green. Unfortunately fluorescence may vary somewhat in shade, or even colour, according to the lamp used, and perhaps even with the observer's colour sense, so the value of the method is at present undetermined.

The Whitefriars glasshouse, just off Fleet Street in London, which made large quantities of decorative glass, including glass designed for William Morris, also made paperweights, but little detailed information about them exists. Specimens dated 1848 exist, as well as one that has the label of the glasshouse under the base.

American paperweights did not appear till after 1851, and the earliest came from the New England Glass Company. Dated specimens of 1852 exist. During the decade which followed they were very popular, and they are still being made today. Usually the decoration of early weights is French-inspired, but with differences which make them identifiable without much difficulty to anyone accustomed to examining old paperweights. The principal manufactories were the New England Glass Company, the Boston and Sandwich Glass Company, and William T. Gillinder.

Reference has already been made to crystallo-ceramie paperweights, known in America as sulphides, the best of which were made by Apsley Pellatt in England. They had their origin in Bohemia, where the first attempts to enclose clay medallions in glass were made in the middle of the eighteenth century, but also in the work of James Tassie of London who made relief portraits of the notabilities of his day in a kind of glass paste which enjoyed considerable esteem in the last quarter of the eighteenth century (above). His work seems to have been well known on the Continent, inspiring Barthélemy Deprez in France to enclose similar portraits in glass, using the Bohemian technique. Sulphides came from Baccarat, Saint-Louis, and Clichy at a later date.

Pellatt patented his process in 1819, his

Above, top :
Medallion portrait of Oliver Cromwell in glass paste by James Tassie, *c.* 1790. Tassie began by reproducing antique carved gems in a kind of glass paste which had the appearance of porcelain. He came to London, where his gems were extremely popular, but he soon turned to making small portraits of celebrities, of which some 500 different examples survive. Tassie supplied Josiah Wedgwood with prototypes for his jasper portrait medallions.

Above, bottom :
Sulphide (crystallo-ceramie) with an unknown portrait, Stourbridge, *c.* 1845. 'Crystallo-ceramie' was the name given to this originally French technique by Apsley Pellatt, who perfected it. Objects of this kind are termed 'sulphides' by the American collectors but the term 'incrustation' is the most appropriate.

cameos being made of 'China clay and super-silicate of potash' inserted into a pocket in a 'gather' of molten glass which was then collapsed on it. Sulphides were widely manufactured during the nineteenth century and up till modern times, not only as paperweights, but for a variety of other purposes. They decorate decanters, mugs, jugs, candlesticks, and so forth, the bases sometimes being cut in addition.

Paperweights and doorstops of heavy bubbled green bottle glass are popular collectors' items today. The interior has a motif of pale green leaves and flowers covered with small silvery bubbles. These are due to the use of chalk, which was picked up on the soft glass in the process of building up the weight in successive layers, and when heated evolved a gas which was trapped under the following layer. Large pear-shaped bubbles were formed by inserting a wire into the molten interior, allowing air to enter, where it expanded as a result of the heat.

Plain glass weights painted on the underside in cold colour are rare, and the so-called Pinchbeck weights, the design press-moulded in metal foil, are not often seen. The former necessarily have to be mounted on some kind of base in order to protect the back. Pinchbeck weights seem once to have been popular, but their production was probably confined to the years around 1850. Some were made by J. and L. Lobmeyr of Vienna, but the origin of most is difficult to conjecture.

Finally it remains to mention Victorian weights with a colour transfer or engraving on the base, which can be found quite frequently. They were made in immense quantities, and are artistically and financially negligible.

Paperweights of all kinds, especially the *millefiori* types, are still being made today by Baccarat and Saint-Louis, and Chinese and Japanese weights copying early types are also well known. French weights from factories of such importance as those named are worth adding to a collection for what they are. Oriental weights are poor in quality, and not worth acquiring.

Modern Bohemian (Czechoslovakian) weights can also be found in many small antique shops, and some are of good quality. Unless the seller has ambitious theories about their origin and date they should not cost more than a few pounds. However, the paperweight collector who is not an expert in his own right would be well advised to buy only from responsible and reputable sources.

Below, left :
Glass with hobnail cutting containing a sulphide, *c.* 1845.

Below, right :
Cylindrical tumbler with cut pillar flutes at the top and lanceolate cutting below. The medallion encloses an inserted moss rose with a butterfly in paperweight technique, Baccarat, *c.* 1848. *Millefiori* and related techniques were not confined to the making of paperweights. Most factories making the latter also turned out a variety of objects such as inkwells, vases, bottles, hand coolers, and many other similarly decorated wares. The French factories in particular excelled in this kind of work.

Nineteenth and Twentieth Century Glass

The end of the eighteenth century in Europe found the art of glass in steady decline. Through the century Venetian glassmakers had tried all kinds of novelties, some of them bizarre, in attempts to revive a flagging trade. The fall of the Venetian Republic took place in 1797, and in the early years of the nineteenth century almost all the glass furnaces were cold, and the guild of glassmakers had been disbanded. It was not until the middle of the nineteenth century that the industry began to revive. The Abbot Zaneth helped to found the Museo Vetrario and a school of design. Nevertheless, Venice sent nothing to the Great Exhibition of 1851, where French and Bohemian glasses were both well represented. The styles of the Renaissance were revived after 1866 by Antonio Salvati (1806–1900), and he was soon followed by others. Work of this kind, however, principally catered for the tourist trade, and it is only more recently that the firms of Barovier and Venini have come to terms with contemporary taste. The modern style in Venice has largely been the work of Ercole Barovier (born 1899), the descendant of a fifteenth-century Muranese glassmaking family, and Paolo Venini (1895–1959). Both are noted for the simplicity of their forms, some of which come from traditional sources, in either colourless or tinted glass. Venini later revived the *millefiori* and *latticinio* techniques, and experimented with surfaces. In 1929, he began his cooperation with the sculptor Napoleone Martinuzzi, constructing plant forms and figures over a metal framework. Some remarkable designs based on plants and fish were created in 1933 by the Swedish potter Tyra Hindgren. Ercole Barovier also introduced many new varieties of glass, particularly addressing his efforts to devising novel surface effects.

At the beginning of the nineteenth century the most fertile source of new ideas and new fashion was Bohemia, although from about 1840 onwards the lead was taken by France. England produced a large variety of decorative glass but, for the most part, in derivative techniques and styles. America specialized in quantity production, often utilizing machinery, until the end of the century, when the remarkable achievements of Louis Comfort Tiffany and Frederick Carder brought American art glass into competition with that of France. The two men had much in common in their aims and productions, but Carder was perhaps technically the more versatile.

By the end of the eighteenth century Bohemia had begun to show a preference for facet cutting in the English manner, often using coloured or cased glass for the purpose. The Romantic movement in art generally revived interest in glass staining, and wheel-engraved depictions of ruined buildings and mountain scenery were typically Romantic themes. These subjects were quite commonly engraved on glasses of all kinds, as were topographical views of cities, and the fashion for decorations of this kind can be equally well seen in paintings on contemporary porcelain in Germany and England. Such work was done by Samuel Mohn (1762–1815), who was at Dresden from 1809 until his death. His son, Gottlob Samuel Mohn (1789–1825), went to Vienna, where he met Anton Kothgasser (1769–1851), who was then a porcelain painter and gilder. Gottlob continued to follow his father's styles, and painted stained glass for the Emperor. The Mohns devised transparent colours for glass painting to take the place of the opacified colours which were formerly employed in decorating German enamelled glass. Kothgasser, whose glasses are much sought after, was employed until 1840 by the Royal Vienna Porcelain Factory, and it must be assumed that he painted glass as a *Hausmaler.* Usually he preferred the *Ranftbecher* on which to work—a tumbler with a thick, fluted base. His work is often signed, sometimes with his address (277, Spanischer Spitalberg, Vienna) added, which reinforces the supposition that he painted glass at home. Kothgasser's colours were brilliant, and he often used the yellow stain of the stained-glass window painters, which was derived from silver. There were many other painters of glass more or less contemporary with Kothgasser who are less well known, but whose work is now collected. Most of them were *Hausmäler* who also painted porcelain. The principal workshops were in Dresden and Vienna, but they also existed elsewhere in Germany.

Very little entirely colourless glass was being made in Bohemia by this time, although clear, colourless glass cased or flashed with coloured

glass and subsequently revealed by cutting is fairly common. Ruby red, derived from either copper or gold, is the most frequent colour, but opaque white, green, blue, amethyst, amber topaz, and a greenish-yellow from uranium, were all being made. To these were added new varieties, such as 'Hyalith' glass from glasshouses owned by the Count von Buquoy, which was made in two colours—sealing-wax red and a dense black. The black variety often imitated Wedgwood's basaltes stoneware. 'Lithyalin' was a marbled glass of several colours made from 1829 by Friedrich Egermann (1777–1864) of Blottendorf. Most glasses of this period belong to what is termed the Biedermeier style in Germany. This was a German version of the late Empire style, which was represented to some extent in England by the styles of the 1820's and 1830's.

The second half of the century was chiefly characterized by enamel painting and revived styles till the rise of the Art Nouveau style, known in Germany as the *Jugendstil*, in Austria as the *Sezession*, in France as *le style moderne* or *le style anglais*, and in Italy as the *stile liberte*, the latter an acknowledgement of the prominent part played by the London firm of Liberty's in promoting it. Art Nouveau was the first coherent style to emerge from the confusion which followed the end of the Empire style in the 1820's. It is a romantic style with its roots in neo-Gothic and the kind of Japanese art which had been fashionable since the 1860's. It is essentially both asymmetrical and curvilinear, with a repertory of ornament largely based on naturally rendered plant forms, especially the lily. In glass, Emile Gallé made an extremely important contribution towards its development, and the iridescent 'Favrile' glass of Louis Tiffany (page 111) was also influential. Gallé was a significant influence on contemporary German glass designing and Lötz Witwe, of the Bohemian factory of Klostermühle, patented a method of iridizing glass in 1873. The technique was later adopted by other Bohemian factories, and iridized glass was being exported by Witwe to North America by 1879.

Among Austrian firms of distinction may be noted the still-existing J. & L. Lobmeyr of Vienna, founded in the 1820's, which in more recent times has specialized in *Tiefschnitt* and *Hochschnitt* engraving of high quality. Important work was done in Vienna by Wilhelm von Eiff (1890–1945), who in his youth had come into contact with René Lalique in Paris. Von Eiff was a wheel engraver who did some distinguished work in *Hochschnitt*, and greatly influenced contemporary glass design in Germany.

In France the beginning of the century saw the production of cut and engraved glass, but new departures were soon in evidence. Opaline glass was at first inspired by the achievements of the Bohemian colour-chemists. The earliest French opaline is almost indistinguishable from the German *Milchglas* when it is white, but it later became more like the 'milk-and-water' glass which the Germans termed *Beinglas* because the opacifying agent was bone ash. The term *opaline* first came into use at Baccarat about 1823. The best opaline was made before 1870, and the earliest examples, made between 1810 and 1820, are in an Empire style, and include such objects as vases and carafes, as well as candlesticks and other domestic utensils. After 1820 the number of forms increased considerably, but quality began slowly to decline, probably because larger quantities were being made to meet an increasing demand. Painted decoration before 1835 was sometimes in cold colour, but after this date enamel colours were the rule.

The commonest colours are the greens and blues, to which sky-blue was added after 1835. An almost opaque white was often used for lampshades. The rare colours are particularly admired. These include the *gorge de pigeon*, translucent and faintly tinged with mauve; the *boules de savon* (soap bubbles) introduced about 1822, opal glasses of several colours with a misty, rainbow-like appearance; the very rare yellow opaline, using antimony as a colouring oxide, which dates from 1810; turquoise, another rare colour, which dates from 1825; and violet, very rare, from 1828. The purple of Cassius yielded pink, the earliest examples being distinctly reddish in tone, but lighter in shade after 1825. Black opaline may be seen occasionally. Opaline glass was manufactured in France at Baccarat, Saint-Louis, Le Creusot and Choisy-le-Roi.

The glasshouse at Choisy was under the

Above, left :
Covered beaker decorated with wheel engraving in the revived Rococo style, Friedrich Egermann (1777–1864), Bohemia, c. 1840. Egermann patented 'Lithyalin' glass and made many types of glass decorated in numerous ways. This beaker is traditionally engraved with a kind of Rococo ornament which differs in form and disposition sufficiently for its 19th-century dating to be immediately obvious.

Below, left :
Flagon of ruby glass, Bohemian, 19th century. The rich colour is due to the employment of reduced copper, i.e., the glass was originally melted in an atmosphere deficient in oxygen but rich in carbon monoxide. The copper is dispersed throughout the glass in minute particles. When the glass is slowly reheated, these become copper-coloured and visible to the naked eye, and in this case the glass becomes the *avventurino* of Murano.

Opposite, left :
Ranftbecher painted with a view of Vienna by Anton Kothgasser, c. 1815. The glass is signed *A.K.* The *Ranftbecher* is a beaker on a thick, slightly protruding base; the derivation of the word is obscure. *Ranft* means 'a crust of bread', or, figuratively, 'an edge or border'.

Opposite, above right :
Goblet of opaque white glass with painted floral decoration, English, probably Stourbridge, c. 1845.

Opposite, below right :
Beaker simulating porcelain with a transfer print of Shakespeare's birthplace, Stourbridge, c. 1840. This beaker employs a method of decoration commonly used for porcelain but infrequent on glass. It was probably made for sale as a souvenir at Stratford-on-Avon not far away. Porcelain souvenirs of this kind had been made since the 1760's, but they are rarely made in glass.

directorship of Georges Bontemps (1779–1884) descendant of the valet of Louis XIV. Choisy was founded about 1820 and closed in 1850. Its director was a glass chemist and technician with a talent for experiment. He introduced the manufacture of cased and flashed glass in the Bohemian manner, and rediscovered the secrets of making *latticinio* and *millefiori* glass. There is a *latticinio* pitcher from this source in the Musée de Sèvres. There is doubt whether Bontemps ever made much use of the *millefiori* technique himself. Choisy undoubtedly made some paperweights, but probably very few. Bontemps published his *Guide de Verrier* in 1868, in which he devotes a chapter to *latticinio* techniques, termed *verres filigraines* (filigree glass) in France.

Millefiori paperweights, and allied types, have been discussed in an earlier chapter, but the pre-eminence of French craftsmen in this field is undoubted. They were also early in the field of automatic and semiautomatic production. A technician named Robinet invented a machine for blowing glass bottles into moulds in 1824, and the moulds were adapted to produce bottles which had decorative moulding in relief. These were ornamented with portraits of historical personages, monks and nuns, buildings, and many other subjects, which are now collected. Many of these bottles were made at Trelon (Nord), a branch of the Baccarat factory. The art of pressing glass into moulds was an American development early in the nineteenth century, but French glasshouses employed these techniques to make excellent reproductions of Irish and English cut glass.

The most important developments, however,

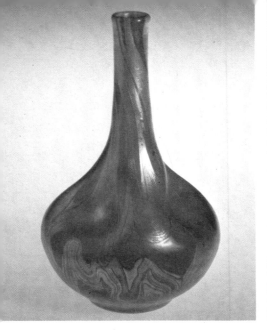

Above, left :
Iridescent vase by Lötz Witwe, Vienna, *c.* 1890. Witwe almost certainly derived his use of this technique from the Viennese firm of Lobmeyr, who were exporting iridized glass to the United States by 1879, where it at once became extremely popular and was used constantly both by Tiffany and by Frederick Carder.

Above, right :
Millefiori vase, Salviati & Co., Venice, *c.* 1895. Antonio Salviati founded the firm that bears his name in 1864, and the Venezia-Murano Company two years later. Both were noted from the first for their revival of old Venetian techniques, as well as close copies of old glass. The Venezia-Murano Company exhibited *millefiori* work which included vases at the Paris Exposition of 1878, but they do not seem to have made paperweights.

Centre :
Vase of clear glass with applied decoration designed by George Thomson in 1952 for the Corning Glass Company.

Bottom :
Scent bottle in the form of an obelisk, crystal glass flashed with ruby and wheel engraved, Bohemia, *c.* 1830. Decorative perfume bottles have long been made in glass, and perfume makers like Guerlain, founded in 1828, commissioned fine quality bottles from noted contemporary designers and manufacturers, which are now collected.

Right :
Vase with iridized surface by Tiffany, who made a notable contribution to Art Nouveau with works such as this in the closing years of the 19th century.

Far right :
Art Nouveau vase of violet glass, Bavaria, second half of the 19th century. The Art Nouveau style became fashionable in Germany rather later than in France and England. Artists associated with the Deutsche Werkstätte, near Dresden, and the Wiener Werkstätte were principally responsible for spreading the style.

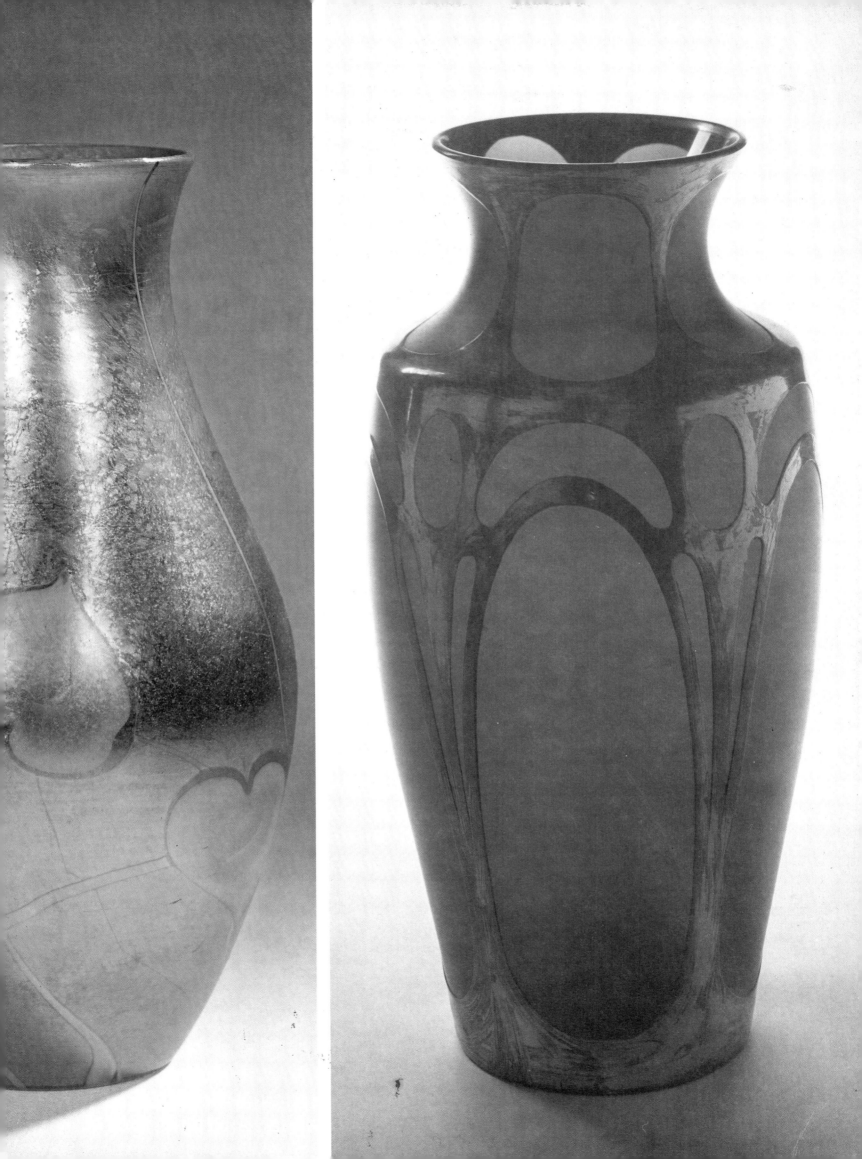

took place in the last quarter of the century, beginning with Emile Gallé (1845–1905) of Nancy, who was one of the moving spirits of Art Nouveau. His father, Charles Gallé, made furniture and faïence, and, inheriting a glasshouse, he added this to his manufactures. Emile Gallé learned the craft of the glassmaker, and then studied the art of design at Weimar. He founded his own glasshouse at Nancy in 1867. Gallé contributed to the Paris Exposition of 1878, and established his reputation by exhibiting a variety of novel techniques, employing the cased glass (*verre doublé*) technique with increasing frequency. He had the advantage of being able to use hydrofluoric acid to remove unwanted glass. By the Exposition of 1889 Japanese influence is obvious, and thenceforward it can fairly be said to have dominated most of Gallé's work. An unusual departure, dating from 1884, are his *verreries parlantes*, each of which has the quotation that inspired it —from poets like Mallarmé or writers such as Victor Hugo—on the glasses themselves. Here Gallé consciously related his work to the ideas of the *Symbolistes*, a school of late nineteenth-century painting which endeavoured to express ideas in form and colour connected with the symbolism of contemporary French poets, Mallarmé especially. The lithography of Odilon Redon and the early work of Gauguin both belong to this movement. Gallé's factory continued after his death until the 1930's, when it seems to have closed. He was among the first to sign his work.

Gallé's styles influenced the work of his pupil Alphonse Reyen, and that of E. Léveillé in Paris. Daum Frères of Nancy closely copied Gallé's techniques, and what is known as *l'école de Nancy* came into existence in 1901. Cased glass similar to that of Gallé was also made at a glasshouse at Sèvres, just outside Paris. Gallé's work had a considerable influence on glass design in the early years of the twentieth century in Belgium, Sweden, and Norway. Several firms produced glass inspired by Gallé by mass-production methods, notably Müller of Lunéville whose work sometimes bears the firm's name.

Between 1867 and 1885 glass inspired by Japanese art, especially that of pottery, was being made by Eugene Rousseau (1827–91). Few specimens have survived, and these are mostly to be found in museums. Rousseau applied metallic oxides to the surface of glass and then cased it with transparent glass which yielded very striking interior colour effects. His glasses were large and massive, sometimes mounted in bronze in the fashion of the time for other objects. His pupil, the E. Léveillé already mentioned, continued his work, and specimens from this hand are more frequently to be found.

Pâte de verre was a revival of a very ancient technique involving the firing of powdered glass in a mould. In this medium Henri Cros

(1840–1907), and his son Jean made reliefs of several colours. Cros carried out his experiments at the Sèvres porcelain factory, and a potter here, Albert Dammouse (1848–1926), started to experiment in 1898 with a substance which had some relationship to the early glassy porcelains, making vessels with floral decoration which are now much admired. Work in *pâte de verre* was done by another potter, François Décorchement, from 1904 onwards. He attracted considerable attention at the Paris Exposition of 1925 with bowls and vases, massive in form, in subdued colours reminiscent of certain hardstones, some with high relief ornament.

Among the nost noteworthy glassworkers of the twentieth century is Maurice Marinot (1882–1960), who originally belonged to the Fauvist movement which included Matisse, Dérain, Vlaminck and Rouault. Marinot abandoned painting in order to work in glass. He was master of many techniques, but his glasses were individually made and are rare. René Lalique (1860–1945) had already achieved fame by 1900, for his contributions to the Art Nouveau style, principally as a designer of jewellery. He began to produce glass in 1902 and experimented with decorative window panels. Coty commissioned him to make small

Above:
Cup and saucer of cut glass mounted in gilt-bronze, French, *c.* 1810.

Opposite, top:
Tazza, wheel engraved with arabesques, France, Clichy-la-Garenne, 1862.

Opposite, below:
Vase of opaque white glass with relief decoration, French, probably Baccarat, *c.* 1845.

Below:
Toilet box of black glass with chrysanthemum decoration by René Lalique, France, 20th century.

perfume *flacons*, and decorative *flacons* in a similar manner were also made at Baccarat for Guerlain. Lalique also made glass in quantity with the aid of press-moulding, as well as individual pieces by the 'lost wax' process, a technique borrowed from bronze-casting, which was also occasionally employed by Frederick Carder at the Steuben glassworks. Lalique had a considerable influence on the Art Deco styles of the 1920's.

The art of glass in nineteenth-century England can, more or less, be said to have started with the repeal of the Glass Excise Act in 1845. This had impeded the development of the industry for more than a century, and had entirely changed the direction in which English glass was developing. Following the repeal, no immediate improvement in the art of glass was perceptible, because taste, just five years before the Great Exhibition of 1851, was at a very low ebb. To begin with, the English manufacturers began to imitate the highly successful Irish cut glass, which had provided the most outstanding examples of this kind of work between 1780 and 1825. Heavy glass, profusely cut, made its appearance, but little glass of merit was shown at the Great Exhibition. Much more tasteful were the painted clear glassware designs commissioned by Henry Cole for Summerley's Art Manufactures in 1847, and the exhibition contained some painted glass versions of Greek pottery (page 104). It also included 'Anglo-Venetian' glass, such as the ice-glass shown by Apsley Pellatt, and *latticinio* wares, as well as threaded glass—objects decorated with coloured glass thread—a great deal of which came from Stourbridge.

Such makers as Davis, Greathead and Green of Birmingham and W. P. H. Richardson of Stourbridge were making decorative glass in a multiplicity of techniques, and in a variety of forms and colours, often with enamelled decoration. Richardson, for instance, did some excellent painting on opaline vases. The influence of Bohemia became increasingly evident in the years following the Exhibition, and in 1851 the *Birmingham Journal*, evidently displeased with the quality of English design, suggested buying a collection of Bohemian glass for the workmen to look at. *The Times* a week later admitted that English manufacturers could not equal those of Bohemia.

But Ruskin had other views, and he stigmatized cut glass as barbarous because instead of exploiting the ductility of the material it merely imitated rock crystal. Cut glass was already losing favour with the public, and Ruskin was the acknowledged arbiter of taste of his period. Not only did the art of decorating glass in this way decline rapidly in consequence, but it has never returned to the favour it enjoyed during the 'Anglo-Irish' period of 1780–1825.

In 1859 Philip Webb designed a set of table glass for Morris, Marshall, Faulk and Com-

pany; Jenkinson of Edinburgh about the same time specialized in the extremely thin blown glass which they called 'mousseline', and James Cooper and Sons of Glasgow were making their 'Clutha' glass, deliberately bubbled and striated, which was designed by Christopher Dresser, all of which were pointing the way to twentieth-century styles.

Christopher Dresser (1834–1904) was an early collector of Japanese art, and visited Japan in 1867, where he assembled a collection of silversmiths' work for Tiffany. As a designer he played a considerable part in the development of Art Nouveau, and some of his glass designs were influenced by those of Gallé. The forms of Clutha glass, however, appear to have been inspired by Roman glass found in excavations.

The nineteenth century was a period of experiment but also one of revival. Under the aegis of Benjamin Richardson of Wordsley, near Stourbridge, John Northwood began experiments towards a revival of cameo cutting, and a faithful reproduction of the Portland Vase (page 25). Eventually he opened his own workshop with the aid of his son and pupils; an example of the work of one of his pupils, George Woodall, is to be found on page 14. This school came to an end soon after 1900.

English manufacturers took up the pressed-glass technique soon after its invention in America in the 1820's, and the industry was at first centred in Birmingham and Stourbridge, although only a few early specimens (usually plates) have survived. Perhaps the most prolific manufacturer of pressed and moulded glass in the nineteenth century was Sowerby and Company of Gateshead-on-Tyne, who employed the mark of a peacock's head in relief. Much of their decorative production was made from slag glass—an opaque glass of variegated colour, so called because slag from iron foundries formed one of the raw materials. They also produced an opal glass that superficially resembled cream-coloured earthenware, or the Worcester ivory porcelain body of the 1870's; from this they made dessert services with moulded decoration (page 92), and many similar wares in the style of pottery. Much, perhaps all, of their wares were marked, and they usually bear the lozenge device signifying registration at the Patent Office, which gives information about the date of manufacture. The period of the greatest popularity of these wares was between 1870 and the end of the century, and all of them are now collected. A number of other firms produced glass of the same kind, including Henry Greener of Sunderland.

The most common colour employed in the nineteenth century was a ruby glass derived from copper, now known as *cranberry glass*. Early specimens often came from Bristol, but later wares, especially crystal or opal glass cased with ruby, were made at Stourbridge, where this colour was particularly favoured. Occasionally the colours were reversed, and opal was cased over cranberry glass. Decorative wares for utilitarian purposes, jugs, decanters, wineglasses, sugar basins, and so on are commonly found in uncased cranberry glass.

Most of the Irish glasshouses had closed by 1840, although one Waterford factory continued until 1857. The demand for facet cutting as the sole form of ornament was diminishing, and the styles of Bohemia were attracting both the English public and its manufacturers.

The twentieth century has seen considerable technical advances, especially in lead glass, which has now become the traditional English type for fine quality work. Among the most noted designers in the modern style is Keith Murray, who produced experimental pieces of glass with simple facet cutting made at the Whitefriars glasshouse. His large vases, dishes, and bowls decorated with flat cutting are perhaps the best known. 'Monart' glass, made at Perth by John Moncrieff, belongs to the Art Deco style. It is noted for marbled colour effects. Somewhat similar glass was made by Schneider in France. Since the last war a flourishing school of free-lance glass engraving has grown up in Britain. Laurence Whistler (born 1912) has done distinguished work as a diamond engraver, to which he has since added stipple engraving.

In America the development of glass pressed into moulds began in the early part of the nineteenth century. The first patent was granted to John Robinson of the Stourbridge Flint Glass Works of Pittsburgh for making door knobs. Deming Jarves, who founded the Boston and Sandwich Glass Company of Sandwich, Massachusetts, in 1827, succeeded in that year in making hollow pressed-glass vessels. So much pressed glass was made here in the early years that 'Sandwich' became a generic term for it. The factory seem to have introduced what is now termed *lacy glass*. This is decorated with Rococo-like scrolls, with a stippled effect between the scrolls that produces an appearance not unlike that of old lace. By 1864 a steam-operated press had been devised, and in 1871 a press with a revolving block carrying multiple moulds made possible the mass production of some objects. Moulds were in two or more parts, depending on the nature of the object. The earlier process necessitated a mould in at least two parts into which a measured quantity of glass was poured, followed by the descent of a plunger to form the interior. In 1865 William Gillinder patented a method of blowing glass automatically into moulds, a process which was subsequently greatly improved.

Production of press-moulded glass was soon on a very large scale, and to begin with most of the patterns were those already familiar on cut and engraved glass. Lacy glass was a new departure, and basket weaves became popular and were sometimes employed for versions in glass of traditional pottery shapes, such as a hen seated on a basket (see above), which occur also in English moulded glass and pottery. Bottles and flasks moulded with decorative patterns representing many subjects and in a wide variety of forms were a major product of a large number of factories, and are avidly collected today. Wheelbarrows, railway carriages, cottages, fire engines, revolvers, cannon, books, boxing gloves, steamboats, and figures of notable personages are examples of some of the forms which supplied the place of the more conventional domestic vessels, which were usually decorated with repetitive moulded patterns. The larger pressed-glass factories such as Hobbs, Brockunier and Company of Wheeling, West Virginia, made enormous quantities of vessels of this kind. It is possible that the fashion was derived from the stoneware bottles made at Lambeth in the early decades of the nineteenth century in forms which were similar but not so great in variety.

The Boston and Sandwich Glass Company made a speciality of cup plates in clear or coloured glass ornamented with a variety of designs. More than 500 different patterns have been recorded. These were employed as cup stands in the days when it was usual to pour tea from the cup into the saucer to cool it, a custom

Hen on nest, press-moulded opaque white glass, New England Glass Co., *c.* 1840. This vessel may originally have been made as a container for eggs. It was popular in Staffordshire pottery in England and exported to the United States, where it was copied in glass. Until the advent of press-moulding, the making of a vessel of this kind would have been both difficult and costly.

Centre:
Comport of lacy glass, probably Sandwich, Massachusetts, *c.* 1835. Pressed glass with a stippled background between the elements of the pattern, termed lacy glass, is now much sought after by American collectors. It has also been reproduced, sometimes from the original moulds.

which was prevalent in polite circles in eighteenth-century England. Some of the original Sandwich moulds are said to be still in existence, and have been used to make reproductions.

Under Deming Jarves's direction the Boston and Sandwich Glass Company made a speciality of wheel engraving and facet cutting, and they produced a certain amount of etched glass. Opaline was introduced about 1830. Elsewhere, towards the end of the nineteenth century, the manufacture of what was termed 'art' glass was started, which might perhaps be better termed 'decorative' glass. This employed some of the advances made during the century in the techniques of colouring glass. One type of art glass, which was called 'Peachblow', was obviously inspired by the eighteenth-century Chinese porcelain glaze known as 'peach bloom', and then much admired. A variation with a mottled effect, also occurring in the case of the Chinese glaze, was called 'Agata', although it bears no resemblance to agate. A glass of pale amber shading into ruby was known as 'Amberina'. In 1885, the Mount Washington Glass Company introduced a glass with a satin finish of greenish yellow shading to a delicate pink, which they called 'Burmese'. The factory patented the colour, and sold a licence to manufacture it to Thomas Webb of Stourbridge, in England, who marketed it under the name of 'Queen's Burmese'. 'Pomona' glass, introduced about the same time by the New England Glass Company of Cambridge, Massachusetts, was a glass partly acid-etched and partly stained to a straw colour.

'Favrile' glass was first marketed in 1893. It was made in the Art Nouveau style by Louis Comfort Tiffany (1848–1933) of New York, who had founded the Tiffany Glass and Decorating Company in 1892. His iridized surface was perhaps inspired by excavated Roman glass, and to some extent by the iridized surfaces of the Austrian firm of Lötz Witwe, who had started to export glass of this kind to North America in 1879. The forms of Favrile glass were, for the most part, the popular floral and foliate forms of the period, but occasional traces of Near Eastern influences in Tiffany's designs arise from visits he made to that part of the world. Tiffany's lampshades (page 99), like those of Emile Gallé, are now very highly valued.

The work of Tiffany inspired Frederick Carder, who became the first manager of the Steuben Glassworks, New York, in 1903, and art director of the Corning Glassworks, which absorbed the Steuben company, from 1918 to 1934. Born in 1864 at Wordsley, near Stourbridge, England, to a family of potters, Carder became designer to Stevens and Williams of Brierley Hill, not far away, at the age of 17 and remained with them till he left for America in 1903. His speciality was an iridized glass which he called 'Aurene', but he experimented very

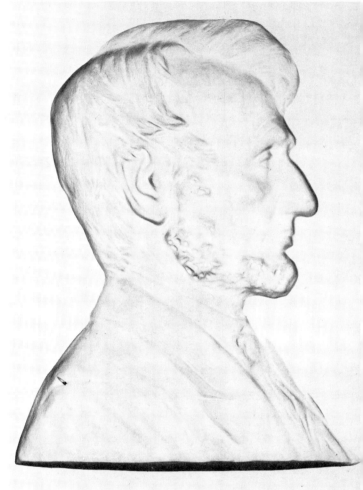

Top right :
Tumbler with a sulphide portrait of Lafayette in the base, American, first half of the 19th century. The Marquis de Lafayette was in charge of the defence of Virginia during the War of Independence. He returned to his native France and became a prominent member of the National Assembly during the Revolution. America never forgot his service to the infant Republic, however, and his name was given to many towns and streets in the United States.

Centre right :
Intaglio portrait of Abraham Lincoln in crystal pressed in an iron mould and satin finished with all surfaces polished, by Frederick Carder, Steuben Glass Co., New York, 20th century.

Bottom right :
Tiger's head by Frederick Carder for the Steuben Glass Co., New York, 20th century. Here Carder has employed an age-old bronze-casting technique. A mould was formed over a wax model and the wax melted out—the so-called lost-wax process.

Below, top :
Stoppered bottle of bubbled glass by Maurice Marinot, Bar-sur-Seine, France, 1929. Marinot specialized, from about 1912 onwards, in individually wrought vases of massive form, often with abstract engraved and etched decoration.

Below, bottom :
Cup wheel engraved with design of three goddesses, designed by J. Horejc and carved by the firm of Stephan Rath Kamenický, Šemov (formerly Stein-schönau), 1924. A distin-guished piece of modern engraving from Czecho-slovakia, formerly Bohemia, which proves the survival of the old Bohemian tradition of fine-quality engraving. The state technical school here educates glassworkers in both modern and traditional techniques.

widely and made glass of several novel and attractive varieties. More recently the Steuben Glass Company has marketed some distinguished wheel-engraved glass by the sculptor Sydney Waugh.

Scandinavia has achieved an enviable reputation since the war for interior design and furnishing, to which the art of glass has made a considerable contribution. A Venetian was working in Sweden towards the end of the sixteenth century, and Swedish glasshouses in the seventeenth and eighteenth centuries were mainly occupied in copying German styles. Most Swedish glass of the eighteenth century is barely distinguishable from German (page 44), and the quality of the engraved work is rarely good. The rise of Swedish glass to the esteem it enjoys at present began with the founding of the Orrefors Glasbruk in 1915. The first couple of years were singularly inauspicious, and it was decided to appoint two art advisers, Simon Gate and Edvard Hald. With their assistance the factory began to produce glass which gradually achieved an international reputation. Their designs were principally figure subjects for engraving which echoed earlier German Baroque and Rococo styles. Orrefors developed a kind of glass flashed with coloured stains, termed 'Graalglas', and a school of glass cutting and engraving was founded. Notable engravers have been Viktor Linstrand, Edvin Öhrström, and Sven Palmquist. The factory made a notable contribution to the Paris Exposition of 1937, and its reputation abroad was considerably enhanced as a result. A factory at Sandvik belonging to Orrefors specializes in table glass, and vases and table glass of excellent quality and design have been produced by another factory at Kosta.

A good deal of crystal glass tableware of excellent quality based on traditional styles has come from Scandinavia generally. The Finnish factories of Karhula Iittala and Notjö Glasbruk have produced well-designed wares of excellent quality, and the modern Danish Holmegaard factory in Copenhagen has made glass notable for the quality of its engraved work, especially that designed by Jacob Bang.

In the twentieth century glass has come increasingly to rely on diamond and wheel engraving as decoration, although both etching and sand blasting are sometimes employed. Sand blasting, which was introduced in 1870, consists of directing a stream of sand particles at a high speed towards the surface to be treated. Usually the glass surface is protected by a stencil, except where it is intended to be eroded. The effect can be controlled by the size of the sand particles used, and the length of time the jet is directed onto any particular spot. The process is normally used for commercial purposes, but decorative glass has occasionally been decorated in this way. Much use has been made in recent years of deliberately induced bubble structures and striations in crystal glass

of good quality, especially by such artists as Maurice Marinot. Forms tend to be massive, and the ductile nature of the material has been deliberately exploited. Asymmetry has almost become the rule, except for table glass. The two ancient categories represented by the *vitrearius* and the *diatretarius* still remain, but the line of demarcation between the two is becoming increasingly blurred.

In the nineteenth century the evolution of glass followed a path which was largely independent of the confusion of styles and the historicism which were important factors in the general degeneration of the decorative arts. This degeneration reached its lowest point in 1851, the time of the Great Exhibition. The reason why glass escaped this may have been that its forms are dictated to a far greater extent than those of other substances by the nature of the material. Objects made of glass must necessarily be formed in a very short time while the material is still very hot. It is therefore unsuitable for ornament in such styles as Gothic, although this could be employed to a limited extent, and in the case of moulded glass a few specimens have survived. There is, however, nothing technically analogous to the way in which porcelain can be cast in liquid form in plaster moulds, to which separately modelled, carefully detailed ornament can subsequently be applied before firing. Nor can glass be worked like metal, which can be sawn, filed, drilled and soldered while cold. In the decoration of glass when cold it is impossible to do more than cut material away, and this considerably modifies what can be done with it.

The many discoveries in physics and chemistry in the nineteenth century made possible new ways of decorating glass and led to greater command over the composition of the metal and therefore of its appearance. They led also to departures from traditional techniques of manufacture and gave rise to novel designs. Of all the materials which had been employed in the decorative arts in past centuries, glass probably benefited the most from the discoveries of the nineteenth century. Although in principle there is little that is not traditional about the manufacturing processes belonging to the *millefiori* paperweight, for example, the way of using these processes was quite new. When we come to the glass of such artists as Gallé, Daum, Tiffany, and others of the same school we have something which would have been impossible at an earlier date.

By the 1870's the various movements away from what had become a *mélange confus* of styles at the time of the Great Exhibition were well established. The Arts and Crafts Movement was solidly based in England. In France, the revolution in the art of painting represented by the Impressionists was gaining ground. The *avant garde* collectors were starting to acquire Japanese art, and this affected contemporary glass in form and decoration, despite the fact

that no Japanese glass existed. Although the beginnings of Art Nouveau are referrable to the 1880's, a good deal of glass made before this date was decorated in styles that foreshadowed Art Nouveau and Emile Gallé was one of the most important influences in the early years of the new style. It was, perhaps, natural that the glassworkers should strike out in new directions, because they were less bound by tradition.

There has always been a wider division between decorative and utilitarian glass than has been the case with porcelain, for example. Domestic glass, largely undecorated or simply decorated with trailing, could be made quickly and cheaply, and after the introduction of such mechanical or semimechanical processes as press-moulding, even more rapidly and at smaller cost. Today, ordinary domestic glass is cheap, and bottles and jars are made to be thrown away. But we have entered a period when materials are relatively cheap and labour expensive, which is the reverse of conditions in the eighteenth and early nineteenth centuries, so that glass decorated by hand has become correspondingly dear.

Pliny, in his *Natural History*, remarks that since the serving maids of Rome took to wearing gold shoe buckles their mistresses had reverted to those made of silver. Because of the ease with which cut glass can be cheaply simulated by press-moulding and the difficulty of distinguishing between hand work and mechanical production at a glance, it has become much less popular with modern manufacturers and their customers, although wheel engraving, which is difficult to reproduce mechanically, and diamond engraving, which is obviously hand work, are still in demand. The latter technique is employed by many studio decorators, and there is a distinct tendency to design decorative glass so that its forms and

decoration are as distant as possible from those made by mechanical processes.

In these days when most objects of domestic utility are made wholly or partially by machine and synthetic materials imitating traditional ones are becoming commonplace, hand work is becoming increasingly valued, whenever it was made. In the field of porcelain, prices comparable with those paid for the rarest antique specimens are sometimes paid for modern work, such as the $50,000 realized a few years ago for a pair of Worcester porcelain birds designed by the late Dorothy Doughty. Modern decorative glass has not yet achieved this kind of esteem, but there can be little doubt that much higher prices than those at present prevailing will be the rule in future.

Above, top:
Panel engraved with a decoration of peacocks, intended to be illuminated from below or behind, by René Lalique, signed in diamond-point engraving. French, 20th century.

Above, bottom:
Two vases of flattened form decorated with fish, by Eugène Rousseau, exhibited at the Paris Exposition of 1878. Rousseau was designer for Appert Frères, Paris, from 1875 to 1878, and also worked in association with Leveillé. His glass is rare, but among the most influential in the modern movement.

125

Index

Acknowledgments

The publishers would like to thank the owners, authorities and trustees of the following collections and museums for their kind permission to reproduce the illustrations in this book:

The American Museum in Britain (photos: Ron Sprules): 21 top, 53 bottom left, 77 bottom left, 88–9, 93 top left, 101 top left, 120–1 both, 121 top;

Museum of Applied Art, Prague (Art Centrum): 12 below left, 16, 33, 37 top right, 57 right, 72, 76 left, 112 top, 124 bottom;

Bethnal Green Museum: 27;

Brighton Pavilion: 7, 98 top;

Bristol City Art Gallery: 17 right, 42 top, 43, 45, 49 top left, 60 top right, 61 both, 65 top right, 67, 68 left, 72–73, 77 right, 81 all, 82–83, 100 right, 105, 114 top left;

British Museum: 9 right, 20 all, 23, 24, 24–5, 26 centre, 28 both, 29 all, 31, 32 both, 34 bottom left, 36 both, 41 right, 44 top, 52 left, 84 top, 88 left top, centre and bottom, 95, 104 bottom right, 117 top;

Ca Rezzonico, Venice: 98 bottom;

Cecil Higgins Art Gallery, Bedford: 13 top left, 15 right, 21 bottom, 30 below, 34 top, 38 bottom, 41 bottom left, 55, 57 bottom left, 59, 60 bottom, 64 bottom, 65 top left, 66, 69 top and centre right, 74 top right, 80, 84 bottom, 96 top left, top right, bottom left, bottom centre;

Christies: 99, 114–5;

City of Liverpool Museums: 12 below right;

Constance Chiswell Collection: 71, 96 bottom right;

Corning Museum of Glass: 121 bottom, 123 top right;

Holbourne of Menstrie Museum, Bath: 48, 49 top right, 62 top, 65 bottom right, 89 top and bottom right, 97 top, 109 left;

Kestner-Museum, Hanover (photos: Hermann Friedrich): 8, 12 top left, 13 below right, 17 left, 35, 37 left, 40 bottom, 41 top left, 44 bottom left and right, 53 top, 56, 57 top left, 58 bottom, 60 top left, 69 bottom right, 76 right, 97 bottom, 112 bottom, 113 bottom left;

Kunstgewerbemuseum, Hamburg: 15 below left;

Metropolitan Museum of Art, New York: 111;

Pilkington's Glass Museum: 10 top left and right, 12 below right, 14 top and bottom, 26 bottom, 34 bottom right, 38 top, 40 top, 42 bottom, 49 bottom right, 58 top, 79, 82, 108 top, 109 right, 114 top right, 122 bottom;

Private Collection: 46 right, 62 bottom left and right, 74 top left, 91 top, 92 top, 103, 114 bottom, 116 top, 118 both, 119 both, 125 top;

Robert Rockwell Collection: 121 centre;

Royal Scottish Museum (photos: Tom Scott): 9 left, 37 bottom, 52 top, 64 top, 65 top centre, 69 bottom left, 77 top left, 114 centre;

Sotheby's: 107;

Stourbridge Corporation: 10 below, 14 centre left and right, 15 top left, 18 both, 19, 25 left, 46 left, 47, 50 all, 51, 63, 68 right, 74 bottom, 85, 90 top, 91 bottom, 108 below, 113 bottom right, 122 top, 123 top left, bottom left and right;

A. Tillman Collection: 39;

Museo Vetrario, Murano (photo: Electa): 87;

Victoria and Albert Museum: 13 top right, 25 right, 30 top, 92 bottom, 93 right top and bottom, 100 left, 101 bottom left and right, 103 left top and bottom, 114 top right, 116 bottom, 117 bottom, 124 above, 125 below.

Jacket Illustrations:
Front: British Museum; *front flap* Cecil Higgins Museum, Bedford; *back* 'Lotus' Punchbowl and Punch glass. Rosenthal Studio Dept (Wilson & Gill), Regent St, London; Dartington ladle. Heal & Son Ltd, Tottenham Court Road, London; *back flap* Stourbridge Corporation.

Endpapers: Mansell Collection, London; *Pages 2–3* Rosenthal Studio 1, Knightsbridge, London; *Page 4* Courtesy of Laurence Whistler and the Cupid Press.

Photographs were kindly provided by the following:

Werner Forman: 26 top, 75;
Angelo Hornak: 27, 39, 53 bottom right, 90 bottom, 98 bottom, 121 centre and bottom, 123 top right;
Bavaria Verlag: 11 all, 15 below left, 115.

Other photographs were specially taken for the book by John Webb, Michael Dyer Associates, Derek Balmer, and the Hawkley Studio.